SHWEDAGON

Golden Pagoda of Myanmar

Women praying in the 1890s.

SHWEDAGON
Golden Pagoda of Myanmar

Elizabeth Moore, Hansjörg Mayer and U Win Pe

Thames and Hudson

The southern entrance in the 1880s.

First published in Great Britain in 1999 by Thames and Hudson Ltd, London

First published in hardcover in the United States of America
by Thames and Hudson Inc., 500 Fifth Avenue, New York, NY 10110

ISBN 0-500-01928-2
Library of Congress Catalog Card Number 98-61826

Editor: Narisa Chakrabongse

Production: Paisarn Piemmettawat

Printed in Thailand by Bangkok Printing Company

Contents

The *stupa* in 1900.

PREFACE

The idea for this book came from a single visit to the Shwedagon, photographs taken on one day, images of the shrine captured in a few hours. The pictures are glimpses, impressions, often of unexpected corners of the Shwedagon. There are richly coloured images of the Buddha and a myriad of other figures. There are flowers, leaves, coconuts, bananas, and other offerings. There are people praying and walking, passing time at the Shwedagon.

No other country has a shrine such as this, ancient, so much a part of today, and guardian for the future. If one thinks of landmarks in cities around the world, none is as lofty and as religious as the Shwedagon. Within Myanmar (known formerly as Burma), one may see the spire of the 11th century Ananda at Pagan, but not from a distance. Mandalay's 19th century palace has its spires and there is Mandalay Hill, but neither has a pinnacle seen from afar.

The Shwedagon has a different character and personality every hour of the day and week of the year. It is an unforgettable vision to see the pagoda across the Royal Lakes at sunset or as a golden shimmer against the black night sky. In the early morning, it is the yellow of the sun burning through the mists. By noon, during the dry season, its glow is too bright to look upon. During the downpours of the monsoon months, it shines in the dullness as sheets of water beat across its surface.

Everyone who has visited Myanmar has a memory of their first visit to the Shwedagon, and for all born in Myanmar, the Shwedagon is part of their life. The pagoda is a meeting place, a shrine, alive with spirits of the past and present. Foreigners admire its beauty, the enveloping atmosphere of worship. Those who go often feel the pull of the Shwedagon: to mount the stairs and pace the platform, feel the smooth stone under one's feet, hear the bells, smell the burning wax and incense, and discover yet another facet of the pagoda. Multiply this combination of feelings many times over, and one begins to understand the way in which the Shwedagon belongs to the people of Myanmar.

Elizabeth Moore

The pagoda in the 1880s showing the 64 encircling shrines in place
and various mythological figures.

A Circumambulation of the Shwedagon

Hansjörg Mayer

with captions by Elizabeth Moore

Offerings to the images of the Buddha include umbrellas or *htis* and flowers. The white and gold on the freshly painted images mirror the colours of the flag, that of the Buddhist *Sangha* or monkhood. There are six stripes recalling the rays that shone from the head of the Buddha. Five can be seen here: brown, gold, red, white, and glowing pink. A sixth, horizontal stripe displays all the colours in a constantly changing hue.

Mural paintings in Daw Pyint's Hall show the story of the Kyaiktyo pagoda, often linked to the Shwedagon. Below elaborate floral woodcarving surrounds figures from several legends. The roof carving imitates the traditional woodcarving motifs but here is cut from metal and painted gold. The pavilion is on the southwest of the platform next to the Arakanese or Rakhine pavilion. It was donated by Daw Pyint, the wife or widow of a government official.

A typical offering, or *gadaw-pwe*.
The silvered coconut resting on a bed of
bananas sits within a metal offering bowl.
A banner including the names of the husband
and wife who made the donation has been
placed with the offering, along with two small
gilded *hti* or umbrellas.

Gilded tin *htis* rest within a pagoda platform before being placed on top of one of the shrines. The concentric rings are fixed to a central pole. The rings, which may be 5, 7, or 9 in number, rise to form a crown similar to that worn by Myanmar kings.

The seat or palin and ornamental backing, the *ta-keh*, are integral elements in a throne for an image of the Buddha. This fine example displays all the traditional elements of the throne finely carved from wood and then gilded.
The signboard below lists the donors.
The alabaster images of the Buddha in the background are seen in detail on page 48, both within a pavilion in the northeast corner of the pagoda platform, east of King Tharawaddy's bell.

15

The large *thabeik* or begging bowl is held by a larger than life-size concrete figure of a holy layman. His white headdress or *konbaung* and white robe distinguish him from a monk, who would wear the traditional reddish brown robes of the *Sangha*. A crow has alighted on the begging bowl, giving an idea of the size of the statue, found on the north side of the pagoda platform.

This engaging pair of elephants is hidden away in the northeast corner of the pagoda. The three-headed elephant may be Indra's elephant Erawan or simply one of the many variations seen in the elephants or *hsin* of the Shwedagon. There are many reasons for donating an elephant: there are associations with events in the life of the historical Buddha, previous lives of the Buddha and Buddhist kingship. When he has tusks, the elephant is the guardian of the south, the direction of the planet Mercury.

One of the few images at the Shwedagon showing the Buddha in a reclining position, in Daw Pwint's Hall next to the Rakhine pavilion on the west of the platform. The auspicious pairing of the Shwedagon and the Kyaiktyo pagodas is seen in a picture fixed on the mural behind the Buddha. The Lord of the Nats, Thagyarmin, is part of the mural. He holds a conch shell with lustral water for the Buddha, standing in the clouds of the celestial realms.

This pavilion, in the southeast corner, is adjacent to the pair
of Buddha's footprints shown on page 43. The brightness of
the freshly painted images shows well here, whereas in fact
the pavilion is dim and rarely visited.

Another reclining image of the Buddha can be found in Daw Pwint's pavilion, on the south side of the main altar. Since the picture was taken, in March 1997, the small seated image at the back, with his beautifully carved throne, has been moved to the centre of the main altar. Among the many small images is the brown-robed figure of Bo Min Kaung, just in front of the reclining image. A devotee has placed an extra cloth around his shoulders; a white umbrella or *hti* shelters him.

Known as Khoo Chein Kan-Ma Kyee's hall, this iron pavilion was built in 1914. It shelters a pagoda, and sixty-four images. Women may make offerings but may not enter the interior cell. The pavilion is on the west side, just south of the west staircase. Just behind the enclosing fence is a small prayer-post or *dagun-daing*, surmounted by a golden *hintha* bird.

The entry to the Shin Ajagona or Izza Ganwa pavilion on the northeast of the pagoda platform. The modern style of the glass mosaic work on the two front pillars contrasts with an older gilded wooden ceiling which can be glimpsed behind the façade and the Victorian lighting fixture. A more recent sign, dated to 1984 or 1346 ME (Myanmar Era), is fastened to the iron grillwork around the door.

Another style of mosaic is seen, also on the façade of the Shin Ajagona shrine. The *kalasa* or vases of plenty are filled with flowers. Low wooden plinths covered with matting offer the devotee a place to sit in meditation or prayer.

The Hall of Great Prosperity on the northwest part of the platform, decorated with a screen of coloured threads for the annual Tabaung festival in March. The glass mosaic pattern on the columns is similar to that of the Shin Ajagona shrine. However, the diamond pattern is slightly larger, and blue insets are used rather than the turquoise and red pieces that fill the diamonds of the Shin Ajagona columns.

A *deva* or spirit figure on the exterior of a pavilion just east of Singu's bell on the northwest of the platform.
The plaque below reads 'Pothios Shipping Co.'.
Devas are commonly placed within the larger category of lords or *nats* but form a separate category of celestial guardians.

One of the many associations on the platform, the hall of the Chinese Merited Association is on the southwest of the platform. The hall is filled with gifts for the festival but is empty at other times of the year. The offerings are for monks, arranged here in the form of a tree. This recalls the legendary wish-granting tree where anything one desired could be plucked from its branches. The sign in front records that it is the anniversary of the Full Moon Day of Tabaung, the year 2540 in the Buddhist Era.

Washbasins found in the southeast corner, near to the shrine of the Shwedagon Bo Bo Gyi. Pilgrims may wash and refresh themselves here; water for drinking is provided in jars at various places around the pagoda.

Further offerings for monks placed within the Chinese Merited Association on the southwest of the platform, arranged for the Tabaung festival. All the items, from towels, to candles and rice, are part of the simple life of the monk. They will be distributed to a group of 108 monks, recalling the 108 auspicious marks of the Buddha.

Bowls within the wish-granting Hall of the Carousel on the southeast part of the platform. Coins or bills tossed into the bowl on the left will bring success in health. If into the bowl on the right, the donor will have success in business. The bowls slowly turn, making the toss more difficult!

The Buddha Konagamana, the second of the three Buddhas of our era preceding Gotama, is seen here on the south side of the Eight-Day Pagoda. The shrine is on the northwest of the platform. Konagamana also rests within the South Adoration Hall facing the southern staircase. *Devas* sit upon an elephant or *hsin* and lion or *chinthe* to either side of the Buddha. These two animals are guardians of the south and southeast, Mercury and Mars, the respective planets of Wednesday until dusk and Tuesday.

Elaborate floral designs flank a central peacock-chest or *tu-yin* motif on one of the many small *stupas* on the platform.

The fierce expression of an ogre
or *bilu* contrasts with the clown-like
figure in the next picture.

The guardian figure sits beneath a dragon-like creature or *naga* on the side of a small pavilion on the southwest part of the pagoda, just west of the south staircase. All the smaller shrines are marked with numbers, such as the '6' fixed by the door on this entryway.

The interior of the Shin Ajagona shrine, filled with *gadaw-pwe* offering bowls filled with coconuts and bananas. The statue of the alchemist, Shin Ajagona, with his eyes of different sizes can just be seen on the far left of the picture – although an umbrella covers his eyes!

Flowers and *tha-bye* or Eugenia leaves nearly cover the popular image inside the Sun and Moon or *Nay-la* shrine on the northwest corner of the platform. The image sits on a plinth with two elephants bestowing lustral water on a rat, associated with the planet Jupiter, the west and Thursday. The outside of the shrine is seen on page 69.

Two of the many shops lining the staircases of the Shwedagon.
Each shop specialises in a different type of figure or offering.

The main image inside the Aung The Sa pavilion, on the northeast corner of the platform.
The shrine is a small one, north and east of the Naung Daw Gyi Stupa. Among the many offerings, an image of Bo Min Kaung can be seen on the right side of the altar.

Images found within the North Adoration Hall, dedicated to the Buddha Gotama. Donation boxes in front offer the pilgrim a choice of uses for any bills placed inside. The two pillars are covered in a small, older style of glass mosaic than the silver mosaic covering the wall behind.

Images lining one side within the Shin Ajagona pavilion. The pavilion occupies an
important position as the southern shrine of the Naung Daw Gyi Stupa. The
clock between the two images is typical of the many timepieces offered throughout the pagoda. The other side of the pavilion is seen on page 46.

Large and small gilded images flank either side of the interior cell of
the Western Adoration Hall, dedicated to Kassapa, the last Buddha
of our era before Gotama.

The smooth and shining face of a bronze image is almost hidden behind a bouquet of umbrellas or *hti*. The image rests within one of many small pavilions on the northwest part of the platform.

Two water-filled footprints of the Buddha rest before a triad of images. Each is cast with the 108 auspicious signs of the Buddha.
A small cup on the left footprint allows pilgrims to make a libation. Off to the right of the picture is the group of images shown on page 19.

A small shrine on the north part of the platform houses an image of the Buddha sheltered by a serpent or *naga*. The form recalls a time after the enlightenment of the Buddha when he sat meditating. A storm arose, and water began to surround the Buddha. The *naga* Mucalinda coiled himself beneath the Buddha and sheltered him with his hood. Although not rare, this depiction is far less common in Myanmar than in Thailand or Cambodia. Three ogre or *bilu* faces below add further protection.

An image of the Buddha on the west side of the Konagamana or Southern Adoration Hall. Although many images are revered, the Shwedagon is different from the famous pagoda of Mandalay, the Mahamuni or Hyapagyi ('great merit or lord'), where one image is revered above all others – the highly revered image of the Lord Buddha said to have been made in a likeness of him. The image was brought to Mandalay from the Arakan or Rakhine region during the time of King Bowdaypaya in 1785 AD.

The opposite side of the Shin Ajagona pavilion from that on page 40. The two most popular forms of renovation for images of the Buddha are seen: gilding and painting with white skin, orange robe, and gilded headband.

Three men meditating in a pavilion on the West Side of the Northern Adoration Hall dedicated to Gotama. Note the photograph of the Kyaiktyo pagoda on the upper left. The hall is not reserved for men, and women regularly pray there as well.

A row of alabaster images of the Buddha, also seen in the background on page 15, within a pavilion in the northeast corner of the pagoda platform, just east of King Tharawaddy's bell. The images are guarded by a grill, but nonetheless have been venerated for the Tabaung festival with fresh orange robes. Much of the alabaster carving of images still takes place around Mandalay in the central part of the country.

Four small images of monks are encased behind glass at the top of a pavilion on the west of the platform, just north of the west staircase. The pavilion, due to its unusual proportions is often referred to as the Pavilion with Tall Pillars. From the platform level, these images can hardly be seen.

An iron figure of an Indian man seen on the east side of a pavilion on the north side of the platform, opposite the Hall of the Weizas, close to the north staircase. U Ya Thi, a pagoda trustee, built the pavilion in the 1920s. It is know by several names. Some call it the Venus pavilion, as this planet is associated with the north. Others refer to it as the Hall of the Buddha's footprint, as there is a large footprint of the Buddha encircled by a *naga* inside the pavilion. (Although these figures were in place in March 1997 when the photographs were taken, by December 1997 they had been removed owing to their colonial association.)

It is also known for the fine gilded woodcarving on the front screen, parts of which are seen in the picture. The screen to the right, fixed to the mirrored column relates the story of the Shwe-hpyin (meaning 'gold' and 'pot') brothers, who became *nats* when the 11th century King Anawratha found several bricks missing from a pagoda at Taungbyon, 15 kilometres north of Mandalay. The king had the brothers executed. They became the *nats* Min-gyi and Min-glay, meaning great and little lord. Their story is celebrated during an annual festival in Wagaung (July-August). A popular part of the story concerns Me U, a beautiful young weaver who refused the attentions of the two brothers. They sent a tiger to devour her, dragging her away from her loom. As a result, Me U also became a *nat*, Taungdaw Thakinma or 'mistress of the hill'.

A bell on the northeast corner of the pagoda platform. In the background is the staircase leading to the upper part of the platform. Its use is reserved for men. In the far distance is the upper part of the Naung Daw Gyi pagoda.

A young pilgrim is striking the bell, accompanied by a friend or brother who has undergone his *shin-byu* or novitiate ceremony to become a monk. He may stay in the monastery for a short time or the rest of his life.

Young pilgrims seen on the southwest corner of the platform, just west of the south stair. The young woman has *thanaka* makeup on her cheeks. Made from the bark of the sandalwood tree, the makeup has astringent properties. The fine skin of Myanmar women is often attributed to its use.

Small pavilions on the southeast part of the platform just next to the Hall of the Carousels seen on page 28. The large floral motif is an example of the decoration on the *anda* or bell of the main *stupa*. It is made up of metal plates and placed in the pavilion for meditation. It is not, as it might seem, removed from the *stupa*, or a mould for making stucco or terracotta examples.

Two young women examine various mementoes on the edge of the platform. Both women are probably unmarried. This is especially noticeable in the young woman on the right, as her hair has been kept long, and is not worn up.

Men and women at prayer in the South Adoration Hall
dedicated to Konagamana, the second Buddha of our era.
The western style 'party dresses' of the two young girls
contrast with the more traditional attire of their mother.
All pilgrims and visitors to the pagoda remove their
footwear out of respect for the Buddha.

A young photographer stands in front of a board displaying examples of his wares. His pride is evident not only in his smile but the signboard whose bright red letters state 'fit for royalty'. Many pilgrims visiting the pagoda enjoy having their picture taken as a souvenir. In the background a number of devotees are seen praying in front of the pavilion housing an image of Thagyarmin, Lord of the Nats, and the territorial guardian of the pagoda, the Shwedagon Bo Bo Gyi.

A monk passes before one of the planetary shrines. This one is dedicated to the moon, so is associated with Monday, the east and the guardian tiger or *kya*. The post is on the northeast sector of the platform. Among the many other figures in the background are three elephants, painted white, supporting a shrine for an image of the Buddha.

Any corner of the pagoda may be sought for prayer, as seen in this picture of a lone man meditating.

This man's brown robe and beads identify him as a member of one of the many meditation sects seen at the Shwedagon. Most members practice individual meditation. There are also meditation groups made up of women, some of whom engage in a particular practice called *Ka Thaing* or looking at the sun.

A sacred Bodhi tree on the southeast corner of the pagoda platform. In Myanmar, it is somewhat unusual to see a father tending a child, but is more common at the Shwedagon as most commonly women are busy making offerings.

Another sacred Bodhi tree, on the southwest corner, with small altars for the days of the week. The sapling from which this tree has grown is believed to have come from the very tree under which the Buddha attained Enlightenment.

Women are seen holding up *tha-bye* or Victory Leaves
in prayer. They are seated within a roped-off area
known as the Ground of Victory. The pavement on
this part of the platform forms a flower design with
ten petals. At its centre is the round white stamen,
a particularly auspicious place for prayer.

A woman holds up an offering in prayer.
She is seated within the Bo Bo Aung Tazaung
or pavilion maintained by the Sasana
Dhamma Rakita Athin or Association. It is
found south of the Shin Ajagona shrine on
the northeast of the platform.

Devotees are gathered within the Ground of Victory on the northwest part of the platform. In addition to the cordon marking this auspicious place for prayer are several large flags of the Buddhist *Sangha* or monkhood.

The intent pose of the woman praying contrasts with the casual posture of the young man at her side, and the younger woman behind her. This freedom of choice and relaxed atmosphere is typical of the Shwedagon at any time of day.

The Shwedagon Bo Bo Gyi, swathed in shawls offered in veneration.
He stands next to Thagyarmin, Lord of the Nats or spirits, in a shrine on the southwest part of the pagoda platform.

Wish-granting stones found in front of Bo Bo Gyi's shrine on the southwest part of the platform. When a prayer is made, the stone is lifted. If it is light, the wish will be granted, if it remains heavy the outcome is doubtful.

Another view of the Bodhi trees on the southwest corner
seen on page 61. The large image of the Buddha is
sheltered by a canopy and decorated with flags of the
Buddhist *Sangha*.

Abundant offerings mark the Sun and Moon or Nay-la shrine on the northwest
corner of the platform. The peacock and hare symbolise the sun and moon,
their medallions framed with the bodies of *nagas* or serpents. The Nay-la shrine is
the most popular of the three *stupas* grouped together here. The image inside is
seen on page 35.

One of the many shops near the staircases
selling flower and umbrella or *hti* offerings.

A *gadaw-pwe* is being offered to Bo Min Kaung.
Although images of him are found throughout the platform,
this, on the northeast corner, is the largest.

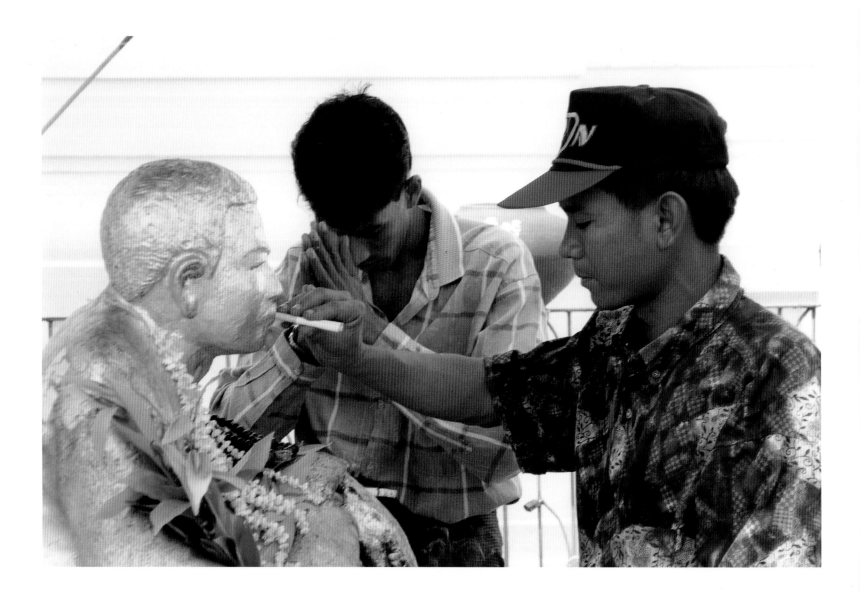

A devotee has offered Bo Min Kaung a cigarette,
which the guardian of the shrine holds to his mouth.

The cigarettes are lit by the guardian, and then added to the many others held by Bo Min Kaung. In contrast, the figure of Bo Bo Aung prefers offerings of betel, a more old-fashioned habit of Myanmar people.

The betel is composed of a leaf, lime paste, and shavings from areca nuts. It is sometimes said that the more recent history of Bo Min Kaung is reflected in his preference for cigarettes rather than betel.

The large image of the Buddha in this shrine sits behind an elaborate glass frame and a circular window. Its shape is considered Chinese, as are the bats on the corners. Known as Chan Mah Phee's Hall, the pavilion is located on the northwest part of the platform. Chan Mah Phee came to Myanmar from the Chinese Straits Settlements of Malay in the late 19th century, although he was born in Amoy (Xiamen). He eventually married a Mon woman, accumulating much wealth through trade and real estate. The structure was built in 1898, with the Chinese name of Fucigong, or 'temple of blessing and compassion'. The exterior woodcarvings are as elaborate as the interior. In addition to the usual flower and Victory leaf offerings are a number of cartons of medicinal drinks, 'Extra Strength Power Gold'.

The main elements of a planetary
shrine are seen here: the post,
a guardian image, an image of the
Buddha receiving lustral water,
and the guardian animal below.
This shrine, on the north, is of the
planet Venus, associated with Friday
and the guinea pig or *pu*.

Another view of the Venus shrine on the north part of the platform. Small cups
and buckets site around a water basin, waiting for pilgrims to bathe the Buddha
with cooling waters. The ground around the shrine is wet with the waters of
earlier offerings.

The planetary shrine of the moon, with its tiger below. The moon is associated with Monday and the east. It is sited immediately south of the East Adoration Hall or Tazaung.

A group of stuccoed and painted *stupas* on the southeast part of the platform. Each is different, in its proportions, shape of the *anda* or bell, and ornamental features.

Stupas on the north part of the platform. The largest was donated by Saw La Paw in 1879. The donor was a *saopha* or chief from part of the eastern Kayah state, called Karenni at that time. In 1883, Saw La Paw joined a group of Shan Saopha to challenge King Thibaw (1878-1885). However, following British annexation in 1885 he joined in the resistance to British rule, until his capital, Sawlon fell in 1889.

The concrete umbrella in the foreground is a commemorative parasol whereas the silver tree behind is a tree of flowers or *pan*, arranged in an offering vase or *kalasa*.

The tall *pyat-that* in the distance marks the Northern Adoration Hall dedicated to the Buddha Gotama. Seen from the west, it is surrounded by a myriad of *pan* trees in *kalasa* vases.

The Small Gilded Pagoda is just east of the Mahabodhi shrine,
whose corner is seen on the left of the picture and again on
page 94. The pagoda is aligned with the central *stupa* and the
Naung Daw Gyi Pagoda.

In the distance is the tall spire of the Naung Daw Gyi Stupa on
the northeast corner of the platform. The picture gives some
sense of the congestion around the Naung Daw Gyi, with
shrines being added at various times over the centuries.

The northwest corner of the platform, just west of the
Hair Washing Well, seen on the right of the picture.
The circle of *stupas* are freshly painted and gilded.
A golden Shan umbrella rises in the centre.

Looking east towards the tiered roof or *pyat-that* of the
Northern Adoration Hall. Small mythical creatures with a
human face and a double-lion body, the *manuthiha*, mark the
corners of several of the small shrines in the foreground.

People throng the wide, marble expanse of the platform.
The Mahabodhi and the Naung Daw Gyi Stupas are seen on the right,
the northeast corner of the platform.

The area north of the east staircase, showing pilgrims circulating in all directions around the main *stupa*. Two large *manuthiha* form part of the platform group of shrines. The sun highlights the angled corners or *kho-nan* on the *stupa* base.

The northeast sector of the platform, with
the Mahabodhi in the distance on the left,
and the Naung Daw Gyi on the right.

The light is strong at mid-day but devotees continue to circulate.
The white *stupa* forms are almost lost against the bright sky, in
contrast to the pink and green *pyat-that* tiers and the yellow and
gold of the small shrines on the left.

On the northeast corner of the platform, another Bodhi tree is seen, with an elaborate *manuthiha*, and another planetary shrine with the animals of the eight days of the week. Two guardians are carrying out repairs to the umbrella or *hti* of one of the small square-celled shrines.

Rows of square-celled pavilions, *kalasa* vases, and gilded *stupas* form protective rings around the main *stupa*. Silver painted *manuthiha* are seen on the corners of one shrine, *devas* flanking its door. At the very bottom of the picture is the upturned trunk of the mythical *pyinsa-rupa*, a composite of five different animals.

The shrines, and particularly the roofs, of the Shwedagon are in constant need of repair. Here a bamboo ladder rests against the roof of a pavilion or *tazaung*.

The distinctive tiered roof or *pyat-that* of the landing pavilion at the top of the north staircase. Renovations are currently underway for this entry.

The Mahabodhi shrine on the northeast part of the platform. Erected in honour of the original Mahabodhi shrine at Bodhgaya in India, the Shwedagon replica dates to this century. It does not reproduce the original, or the Mahabodi temple at Pagan built in the early 13th century, even though in the 12th century, Myanmar architects had carried out repairs to the Mahabodhi at Bodhgaya.

The Naung Daw Gyi Stupa on the
northeast corner of the pagoda platform.
It was here that the Sacred Hairs of the
Buddha are said to have rested when they
first arrived at the Shwedagon. Its form is
said to preserve the original shape of the
main *stupa*.

The northeast corner of the main *stupa* is marked by the planetary post of the Sun, dedicated to the mythical bird, the *galon*, the northeast direction and Sunday.

Just north of the east stair, the planetary shrine in the foreground is that of the Moon, associated with Monday, the east, and the tiger. Guardians are carrying out repairs on the upper level of the base.

An array of images of the Buddha
inside the North Adoration Hall
dedicated to the Buddha Gotama.
The flowing curves of their robes, and
rich gold contrast with the angled
facets of the silvery mosaic mirror-
work on the wall behind.

The history of the Shwedagon begins with legends dating it long before the birth of
the Buddha Gotama in the 6th century BC. Its architecture is a rich array of pavilions
and *stupas* covering the pagoda compound on the summit of Singuttara Hill.
The golden curve of the main *stupa* is seen here, looking across the Royal Lakes.

Shwedagon: its History and Architecture

Elizabeth Moore

Each of the approaches to the platform is unique. Here the staircase is marked by a series of *pyat-that* or tiered roofs. The main *stupa* is seen here from the north. Elephants encircle the fountain in the park at its base.

Page 103
Top left: The high-rise buildings of downtown Yangon are seen south of the Shwedagon, the new Maha Vijaya pagoda is on the left, immediately south of the Shwedagon.
Below left: This aerial view from the NE highlights the separation of the Naung Daw Gyi and the northern portion of the platform, by the wide circumambulatory walkway around the main *stupa*.
Right: The form of the *stupa* seems to change according to distance and the time of day.

The Approach

The Shwedagon is very much a part of the city of Yangon (Rangoon). The Shwedagon Hill is north of the older and busier waterfront area. The north and west stairs are protected from the traffic by parks. When driving along Pye (Prome) Road, there is a magnificent view of the main pagoda. Trees mask many of the lower pavilions, leaving the Shwedagon alone, silhouetted against the sky. Close to the pagoda on the east is a maze of streets, the markets of Bahan. The road then rises, getting steeper as it moves up the lower edges of the hill. It is filled with shops selling images and donations, like the stalls that line the covered staircases. The southern stair, the traditional entry and still the most common, opens directly onto the intersection of three large streets leading ultimately to the port. Cars and pedestrians compete for road space at the changing signals of the traffic lights. Once safely across, pilgrims pause as they slip off their shoes and begin the ascent to the pagoda platform. Many tourists arrive by taxi and are deposited in the parking lot halfway up the southern stair. While a few steps have been saved, they miss the experience of moving between the two thirty-foot high mythical lions, *chinthe*, which flank the lowest set of stairs.

The southern entry has changed and been enlarged over the years. This continues today although the pace of change has always been great, given the constant donations to the pagoda. For example, in 1855, the brick towers were unpainted, and although two guardians sat on either side of the stair, the lions were not yet in place. By the 1870s the wooden arch over the stairs had been replaced by a wide curved masonry arch, and by the 1890s the large *chinthe* had been added. Now, as in the past, the Shwedagon Pagoda Road is lined with monasteries, *kyaung*, and rest houses, *zayats*. Until 1928, there was a moat halfway up the southern stair, crossed by a wooden drawbridge. This is now covered with concrete.

The western staircase is longer than the southern one. It was closed for a long period of military use under British rule. It re-opened in 1930 but then was damaged in a fire the next year. The *tazaung* at the head of this entrance has the typical tiered roof, *pyat-that*. The shrine, built in 1935, is called the 'Two-Pice Tazaung' [11]. *Pice* were small copper coins worth about one and half penny donated by Yangon shopkeepers.

The Shwedagon dominates a hanging, a popular modern souvenir, made of pressed felt stretched between two thin wooden rods.

Each shop specialises in certain wares: some display images and laminated cards of the Buddha together with those of Shin Upako and Bo Min Kaung; others finely carved frames, or a range of photographs, paintings on glass, and offering vessels.

Shops line several staircases leading up to the Shwedagon. They sell a variety of images and pictures. There are papier maché owls, large and small. A male and female pair bring good luck. Among many other animals are sets of eight associated with the eight planets. There are fragrant sandalwood images of the Buddha, wise monks (*shin*), territorial and ancestral spirits (*bo bo*), occult masters (*weiza*), and alchemists (*zawgyis*). There are images of *nats* or spirits. Some are part of the so-called 'Thirty-Seven Nats', codified by an 11th century ruler of Pagan. One of the Thirty-Seven, Myin Byu Shin, is identified by a white horse hung on several of the sacred trees on the perimeter of the platform. Western literature has tended to concentrate on the Thirty-Seven, historical figures that died a 'green' or early and often tragic death. Many other *nats* exist, however, apart from the Thirty-Seven.

Two popular female *nats* are Pegu Mae Daw, the 'royal mother of Pegu' and Thurathai, from the Hindu goddess Sarasvati, consort of the god Brahma. Pegu Mae Daw's buffalo headdress identifies her. It recalls a human mother's thanks to a she-cow that raised her son and then sacrificed her life for him. Thurathati, one of the Thirty-Seven, sits upon Brahma's animal vehicle, the goose. She holds a book, guardian of wisdom and learning. The Lord of the Nats, Sakka or Thagyarmin, also evolved from a Hindu deity, Indra. At the Shwedagon he stands in a pavilion on the southwest of the platform, to the right of the Shwedagon Bo Bo Gyi, the territorial guardian spirit. Thagyarmin and Bo Bo Gyi are swathed in shawls, a form of offering shared with other, lower, *nat* images. Although Thagyarmin and Bo Bo Gyi are *nats*, they inhabit a higher celestial realm than the Thirty-Seven.

A woman makes an offering at the planetary post for those born on a Monday.

Planets and the order of the platform

Most Burmese people cannot remember the first time they visited the Shwedagon. When asked about their last visit, it is usually to the planetary shrine associated with the day of the week on which they were born. Today, each shrine has a post, a sign with the name of the day, an image of the Buddha, and an animal. In the past, the posts stood next to shrines. The Sun shrine for Sunday-born has a mythical bird, the *garuda* or *galon*. The Moon shrine for Monday-born carries a tiger or *kya*. Mars for Tuesday-born has another mythical animal, the lion or *chinthe*. Wednesday is divided into two parts. If your birthday is before six o'clock in the evening, your Mercury post has an elephant, *hsin*. If after six, the elephant is also *hsin* but has no tusks, a much fiercer being. This belongs to the path of Rahu as he traverses the sky in relation to the changing positions of the Sun and the Moon. Jupiter is Thursday's planet, with a rat, *kwet*. This can be difficult to distinguish from the Venus post for Friday's guinea pig, *pu*. Saturn is the planet of Saturday, its post carrying a serpent or *naga*, guardian of the waters of the earth. The placement of a shrine, as with the timing of a festival or ceremony, depends upon the planets, the directions and days.

It is impossible to make 'sense' of the Shwedagon platform. There is no symmetry or grouping of shrines, and no chronological sequence or spread. This would allow one to identify one part or another as being older. One exception is the north side of the platform. The shrines here are linked to the pagoda's founding and this may have been the first part of the hill to be built on. The platform today is rectangular, but would form a square without the north sector. The main *stupa*, now off-set, would then sit in the centre.

Alignment was also not a priority. Only the eastern staircase faces its large Devotional Hall or *tazaung*. Nor are the Devotional Halls cardinally aligned. There is one on each face of the pagoda, but these do not open due east, west, north or south. The majority of the smaller shrines look toward the main pagoda, but not all. One cannot understand the platform chronologically or in directional terms.

The key elements of the Shwedagon are its images and its offerings. Offerings may be from individuals, associations (*athin*), the Buddhist Sangha, the government authorities, or a combination of all of these. Images may be of the Buddha or spirit figures. An understanding of these different aspects does not lie in their inter-relationship but their co-existence.

A devotee might visit his or her birthday shrine, or that of one's mother, father, or relatives. Or one might choose to visit the shrine of a particular day to ensure the successful outcome of an event on that day. Or the visit might be commemorative, of a happy or tragic event. While at first sight the mix of anthropomorphic and zoomorphic aspects, planetary influences, and directionality might seem unusual, it is typical of Myanmar Buddhism. Both the rich Buddhist tradition and the iconography of the *nats* combine zoomorphic and anthropomorphic features. The outcome of stories is often affected by planetary and directional influences. Other Buddhist countries in Southeast Asia have planets and guardian animals associated with days. For example, in Cambodia, the Sun is the planet of Sunday but the animal is a lion, not a *garuda*. The *garuda* is instead associated with Rahu, but not linked to a day. Jupiter is the planet of Thursday but the animal is a donkey, not a rat.

In addition to the day of the week shrines around the base of the main *stupa*, there is the 'Eight Day Pagoda' [17], located near a large Bodhi tree planted by a pagoda trustee in 1901. Images of the Buddha occupy some niches while others hold the animals associated with the planets. The ninth aspect, Kate, occupies the centre, and rides on the *pyinsa-rupa*. This creature combines the most beautiful or striking features of five animals of the air, the land, and the sea. The *pyinsa-rupa* has the tusks and trunk of the elephant, the antlers and legs of the deer, the body of a serpent or *naga* (some say the body and tail of the gudgeon or *nya-gyin* fish), the mane of the lion, and the wings of the *hintha*, a mythical bird. The eight planets and animals carry further associations: honour and position; longevity; kingdom; inauspiciousness; wealth; power and glory; permanence; grace and splendor. Thus, depending on one's birth day, different planetary shrines might be visited to propitiate these qualities.

Crowds fill the pagoda platform during one of the many festivals of the year.

A young boy is carried on the shoulders of one of his relatives during his Shin-byu ceremony. He sheds the trappings of everyday life and enters the monastery. He may stay only a few days or may dedicate his life to the *Sangha*.

Direction	Day	Planet	Animal	Burmese name
NE	Sunday	Sun	Mythic Bird	Galon
E	Monday	Moon	Tiger	Kya
SE	Tuesday	Mars	Lion	Chinthe
S	Wednesday (until sunset)	Mercury	Elephant	Hsin
SW	Saturday	Saturn	Serpent	Naga
W	Thursday	Jupiter	Rat	Kwet
NW	Wednesday (at sunset)	Rahu(causes eclipses)	Tuskless Elephant	
N	Friday	Venus	Guinea Pig	Pu

Just as one day of the week follows another, and just as the planets are arrayed in the sky, nothing takes place in isolation. Both time and space must be considered. The *sayadaw* or chief abbot who advises on all matters relating to the platform must be able to understand the many dimensions that affect a single event. If an act related to the moon is foreseen, the placement of the sun at that moment must also be known. The moon orbits the earth, the planet Rahu. Mars, Mercury, Saturn, Jupiter and Venus are the other planets of the days of the week – all orbitting the sun.

It can be seen how a whole series of movements must be taken into account, all of which are fluid. When this is applied to making 'sense' of the platform, it is apparent that ideas like linear chronology and four or eight directions are simplistic. An intricate system that has little or nothing to do with linear time has determined the location of shrines. One need not know the concept in its fullness to appreciate the Shwedagon. Nonetheless, an understanding of the significance of the pagoda requires a sense of how change, time, and space operate simultaneously within Myanmar belief. This is not 'astrology', but a complex multi-dimensional system to ensure that human action takes place in harmony with the universe.

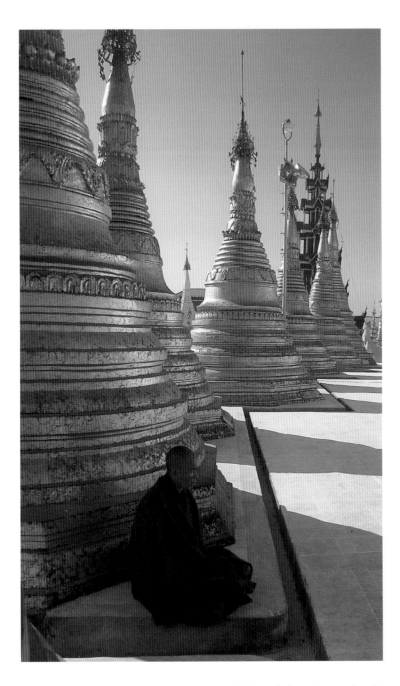

There are many 'secret' places on the upper platform, sheltered areas closed in by a cluster of pavilions. But then one turns a corner and is once again caught up in the wide and beautiful expanses around the main *stupa*. Its curves provide a pleasing contrast of forms for contemplation. (Women are not allowed on the upper platform and men have to have a pass)

The *Sangha* or monkhood is vital in the maintenance of Buddhism. Wise monks at monasteries not only teach, but care for the community. They also play a role in protecting the cultural heritage, for most *sayadaws* possess valuable collections of local images and other archaeological material. In this way they encourage local pride and protection of the cultural heritage.

1. Landing of the Southern Stairway

2. Southern Tazaung – Konagama Adoration Hall

3. Planetary post for Wednesday-born

4. Chinese Merited Association Prayer Pavilion

5. Shrine of the Sun and Moon

6. Arakanese Prayer Pavilion

7. Bo-Bo Gyi, Guardian Nat of the Pagoda

8. Prayer Post

9. Prayer Halls

10. Figures of Sakka, King of the Nats and Mai Lamu

11. Two-pice Tazaung of the Western Stairway

12. Western Tazaung – Kassapa Adoration Hall

13. Low Pavilion

14. Pavilion with tall columns

15. Pavilion with long roof

16. U Po Thaung's Hall

17. Eight Day Pagoda

18. Singu Min Bell Pavilion

19. Shin Saw Bu (Wonder-Working Image) Pavilion

20. Northwest Courtyard

21. Chan Mah Pee's Hall

22. Hall of the Buddha's Footprint

23. Northern Stairway

24. Maha Bodhi

25. Zedi Yangana Association

26. Hair Washing Well

27. Northern Tazaung – Gottama Adoration Hall

28. Small Gilded pagoda

29. Strand Market Two-pice Pavilion

30. Shin Ajagona Pavilion

31. Naung Daw Gyi (Elder Brother) Pagoda

32. King Dhammaceti Stone Inscriptions

33. King Tharawaddy's Bell Pavilion

34. Small Pavilion with interior woodcarving

35. King Mindon's Hti and Bo Bo Aung Shrine

36. Shan Umbrellas

37. Eastern Tazaung – Kakusandha Adoration Hall

38. Eastern Stairway

39. U Nyo Pavilion

40. Prayer Posts with Arahat and Hamsa

41. Sacred Banyan Tree

42. Office of the Pagoda Trustees

43. Fertility Shrine

44. Hall of the Carousel

45. Stairs to the Upper Platform

46. Ruby-eyed Buddha (Tawa-gu) Image Shrine

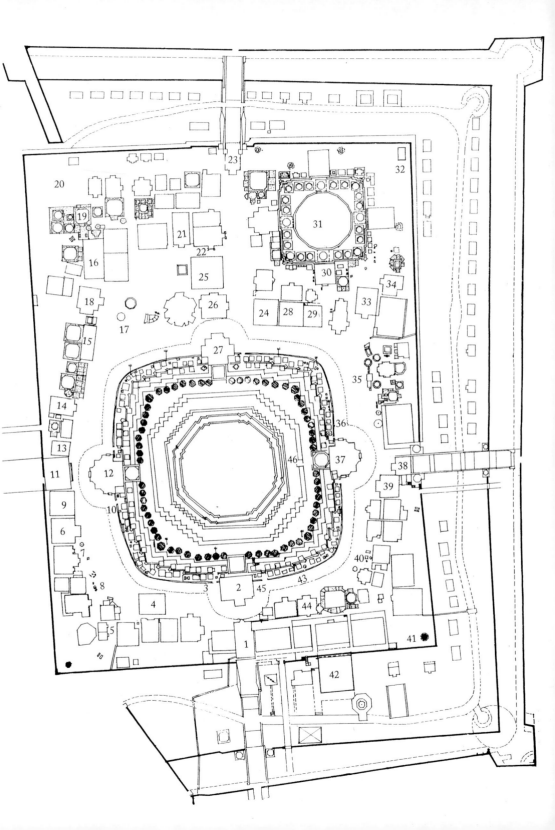

Images of the Buddha and the Jatakas on the platform

The four devotional halls or *tazaung* on each side of the *stupa* base are resting-places during the rains. People wait out the downpours in pavilions on the outer edge of the walkway as well, but inside the *tazaungs* the atmosphere is lively and intimate. Some devotees enter a pavilion, pray, bow three times and leave. Others offer flowers. A rack of beads may be set up near the front, and some, mostly men, pray with these. The halls glitter with silver mirrors and gold tracery. Each has been newly fitted out with a large screen video, all of which display the image of the Ruby-eyed Buddha [46]. The shrine of the Ruby-eyed Buddha, on the upper platform, is out of bounds for women. Today women often pray before the videos. Historically, the Ruby-eyed Buddha shrine, built in 1852, covers the spot where Major Fraser of the British Royal Engineers excavated a tunnel into the pagoda. A Mon, U Taw Lay (1776-1869) was responsible for covering up the hole, and then building the shrine. However, many other beliefs are also associated with this image.

Each of the cardinal *tazaung* is dedicated to one of the four Buddhas of this era or *kappa*. The Southern Tazaung [2] is dedicated to Konagamana, the second Buddha of this era. It has always been elaborate, although its bright form today contrasts with the wooden structure of the 1850s. The Western Tazaung is dedicated to Kassapa [12], the third Buddha of this era. Mythical creatures half-human, half-bird *kinnaya* are carved on the columns. There are male *kinnara* and female *kinnari*. The bright glass mosaics on the other columns overshadow the small gilded figures but they are important reminders of the 550 previous lives of the Buddha, the *jataka*s, where many *kinnaya* stories are found.

The Northern Tazaung [27] is dedicated to the last Buddha of our era, the 6th century BC Gotama. At the base of the northern staircase, to the west, is the Arzani Kone, the mausoleum of Bogyoke Aung San and the other martyrs of the country's independence. The staircase has rail tracks for transporting heavy materials up the hill. The banisters, with crocodiles and ogres, are like those built by Queen Shin Saw Bu in the 15th century. The so-called Thway-say-kan, literally 'blood washing tank', can be seen from this staircase. A strategic point in the First Anglo-Burmese War, Burmese soldiers used it to wash the blood from their swords. King Kyanzittha in the 11th century also used the tank to wash the blood from weapons during the taking of the city of Thaton. At the top of the staircase, the pagoda may be clearly seen, as the landing is a long way from the main *stupa* – the other landings are nearly at its base.

The Ruby-eyed or Mya Shin Buddha on the Upper Platform. Evening devotions in front of the Ruby-eyed Buddha Shrine during the Festival of Lights, at the end of Tha Din Gyut, the October–November lunar month festival welcoming the return of the Lord Buddha to earth following his teaching to his mother in Heaven.

The eastern staircase is the longest and often the busiest. Heavy damage was inflicted on the staircase during the Second Anglo-Burmese War when the British used it as an attack route. The Eastern Tazaung honours Kakusandha [38], the first Buddha of our era. The Queen of King Tharawaddy built a shrine on this spot in the 19th century. It was renovated several times before being destroyed in the 1931 fire. It has been restored since, most extensively in 1968. An image in the central niche depicts the Buddha seated with legs folded, but with the right palm up rather than down on his knee. This posture is repeated on three of the four main images in the shrine.

Scenes from the life of Gotama are found in many of the Shwedagon's pavilions. Typical episodes include: his birth as a prince; his viewing of a sick man, an old man, a dead man and a monk; his departure from the palace to become an ascetic; his renunciation of fasting as the path to enlightenment; his achievement of enlightenment through meditation under a sacred tree; his teaching; and his achievement of non-being or Nirvana. Daw Pwint's pavilion on the southwest part of the pagoda platform shelters a 28-foot long reclining figure of the Buddha. There are also images of his brother Ananda, and his two disciples Shin Ariputta and Shin Moggalana. Paintings recall the founding of the Kyaiktyo pagoda near Thaton. Photographs of the pavilion from the 1970s show that painting of the mural behind the reclining image of the Buddha had already been painted, although not those of the Kyaiktyo. At U Po Thaung's Hall [16] panels carved by U Ba Thin relate the story of King Asoka's missions spreading Buddhism. A trustee of the pagoda and a land officer in the Yangon Development Trust, U Po Thaung built the pavilion in 1923. In U Nyo's pavilion [39] glass mosaic pillars reflect images of the Buddha. The shrine has five gilt spires and panels with the story of the Buddha.

References to the *jatakas* are seen at many of the pagoda's shrines. Among these are stories of birds, both the *kinnaya* and the *hintha*. The Buddha often used *kinnaya* to teach about honesty, for they are so loathe to tell lies that they often remain silent. In the Canda Kinnara Jataka a king shot a *kinnara* in order to possess a *kinnari* he loved. The Bodhisattva Sakka, however, knew of the female bird's fidelity to her mate, and revived the dead *kinnaya*. The two lovers were thus reunited.

The Atthasadda Jataka tells of a king who heard eight terrible sounds in the middle of the night. In the Myanmar version of this *jataka* one of the sounds is that of a *kinnari* who longs for her mate. *Kinnaya* traditionally were carved on the corners of the coffin for the cremation of a monk. At the courts of the 18th-19th century Konbaung kings, *kinnaya* were often carved on the sides of the throne. They were a reminder of the loyalty of the king to his people and also of the Buddha, for *kinnaya* danced in the celebrations that followed His Enlightenment. Today they are a popular symbol of wedded bliss, seen on everything from lacquerware to greeting cards. This is not a new trend, for beautifully carved *kinnaya* decorated the wood-carving in the *taung-pan* or corner floral design of the *pyat-that* over *tazaung* in the late 19th century.

Hintha birds are seen on prayer-posts or *dagun-daing* at the Shwedagon's *Hti* or umbrella shrine [35]. This has concrete models of the *htis* of King Mindon, offered 1871, and the smaller umbrella, donated in 1774 by King Hsin-byu-shin. Prayer-posts are placed around the shrine. Some prayer-posts are topped with a *hti*, a *pyat-that*, and others with animals, occasionally an elephant but more often a bird, the *hintha*. The *hintha* is often called a sacred goose, but in Myanmar it refers to a Brahminy or Mandarin duck, the *wunbe*. The word *wunbe* is found at Pagan on inscriptions identifying paintings of the *jatakas*. Amongst the Mon peoples, the *hintha* has always been distinct from the *wunbe*. Mon chronicles of Pegu describe a visit of the Buddha to the site of the future city, declaring that it would be known as Hanthawaddy, the place of the *hinthas*.

The Javana Hamsa Jataka describes a time when the Buddha was a king of the *hinthas*. He flew in a race against the sun, being praised for his speed by the human king. The *hintha* king answered that this was nothing compared to the passing of a human lifetime. So great was his fear of death that the human king fell unconscious to the ground upon hearing these words. The king's fear spread to his people, causing panic. Eventually the king returned to the *hintha* king, who advised him to abide by the ten laws of kingship, especially charity. It is in memory of the wisdom of the *hintha* that the bird is placed at the summit of prayer posts throughout Myanmar.

The Sulahantha Jataka recalls a hunter who captures the *hintha* king. The earthly king, however, takes pity on the *hintha* when he sees the ruby-coloured blood of the bird on the hunter's net used to snare the creature. In compassion, the human king frees the bird. The *hintha* became a popular reference to charity for the kings, and one sees miniature prayer posts topped with a ruby-studded *hintha*. Thus the stories of the *hintha*, like the *kinnaya*, and like the Shwedagon, have royal as well as religious aspects.

While the main *stupa* dominates the Upper Platform, the many small *stupas* and the prayer posts (*dagun-daing*) contribute to the Shwedagon's extraordinary architectural and ritual atmosphere. Although prayer, offerings and other devotions are communal, many pilgrims come alone to pay homage and meditate.

The *Sangha*, the monastic community, not only protects and propagates the teachings of the Lord Buddha, they also provide an exemplary moral code, one respected not only by Myanmar Buddhists, but the various Christian sects as well.

Types of Buddhism

The Buddhism of Myanmar is Theravadan, instituted as the state religion in the 11th century by King Anawratha of Pagan. The city of Pagan, in the central arid zone of Myanmar, was the centre of religious and royal power from at least the 9-13th century. Earlier Buddhist worship is traditionally recorded in Myanmar as Ari, possibly a Mahayanist or Tantric sect. Mahayanist statues of Bodhisattvas have been recovered from the 1st-5th century Pyu site of Srikshetra, located midway between Yangon and Pagan. Legend records the coming of Buddhism to Myanmar in the 3rd century BC. This may be accurate. Archaeologically, however, it is only from the early centuries AD that dateable artefacts have been found that show the incorporation of Indic rituals, both Buddhist and Hindu, into the existing religions of Myanmar.

Theravadan practice, or 'Way of the Elders', is the set of precepts and practices established after the lifetime of the Buddha Gotama in the 6th century BC. Mahayanists of the 3rd century AD referred to it as Hinayana or the 'Lesser Way'. Within Theravadan belief, Gotama is the sole Buddha of our era with the future Buddha being Mettaya. Ari Mettaya plays a key role in Myanmar Buddhism. His importance within the religion ranges historically from temples at Pagan to present-day practices associated with particular images at the Shwedagon.

The Bodhisattva is a being who has attained enlightenment but delays the attainment of Nirvana to help others achieve salvation. While Bodhisattvas are found in Theravadan Buddhist sects, they are more closely associated with Mahayanist practice. In Mahayana Buddhism, the Buddha Gotama is one of many Bodhisattvas to have attained enlightenment. The emphasis is more on the long path needed to obtain enlightenment. The many examples of those that succeeded, both Bodhisattvas and Buddhas, offer hope for one's own enlightenment in this lifetime or the next reincarnation.

The term Tantric is a broad one, and is used generally to indicate the use of ritual chants and practices which will ensure enlightenment in this lifetime. It can be applied to either Hindu or Buddhist practice. In traditional Myanmar history it is used in a derogatory sense to describe mural paintings of the forest-dwelling sects of Pagan, and the licentious behaviour assigned to the Ari. As little direct evidence of the Ari exists, the negative aura surrounding them may simply be the produce of Anawratha's efforts to legitimise his reign with the full support of the Theravadan monks or Sangha.

Anawratha's institution of Theravadan Buddhism is linked to his capture of the Mon city of Thaton in southern Myanmar. The Mon king and his court were brought to the northern capital of Pagan, traditionally ruled by Burmese peoples who absorbed the earlier Pyu race. The central contribution of the Mon peoples to the development of Pagan is seen also in the history of the Shwedagon. The taking of Thaton was critical in the establishment of Theravadan kingship at Pagan, for the Mons brought three sets of the sacred texts, the Tripitaka or 'Three baskets' (the Buddha; the law, *Dhamma*; and the monastic community, the *Sangha*).

Devotees for the Festival of Lights, a beautiful and tranquil festival in the October-November lunar month. Candles adorn the shrines, their collective light beckoning and welcoming the return of the Lord Buddha.

The Bhumispara or Mahavijaya *mudra* has dominated Myanmar images of the Buddha from the earliest period of Buddhism, the Pyu period. Some authors have explained this, saying the image form is akin to the *stupa*. However in many respects it depicts the most important event in the life of the Buddha, the moments just before he attained Enlightenment and Victory over the forces of the demon Mara. Thus its popularity may reflects its importance, an episode that lead the Buddha into a life of teaching.

The 28 Buddhas and the Four Buddhas of our Era

These main episodes in the life of the Buddha Gotama are shared with Buddhas of previous eras. In Myanmar there are 28 previous Buddhas, although it is often said that there are as many Buddhas as sands in the river Ganges. The 24 who predicted the coming of the Buddha Gotama begin with the Buddha Dipankara, but the 28 Buddhas of Myanmar, include three earlier Buddhas, who did not predict the coming of Gotama: Tanghangkara, Medhankara, and Sarangkara. Within our *kappa*, the Buddhakappa, the last three before Gotama – Kakusandha, Konagamana, and Kassapa – make 27, with Gotama being the 28th. The last three have relics enshrined at the Shwedagon: the walking stick of Kakusandha, the water filter of Konagamana and the robe of Kassapa. They are associated with the Sule, Botataung and Hmawbi pagodas around Yangon. The image of Dipankara is seen at the Eight-Day Pagoda that has images of eight of the previous 28 Buddhas. Dipankara is on the southeast, shown holding a small image of the Buddha Gotama.

Apart from the relics, there are a number of ways to distinguish the different Buddhas. The main episodes of their lives are the same, with birth as a prince or a brahmin, marrying and having a child, seeing the four signs, the Great Departure, fasting, enlightenment, teaching and then the attainment of Nirvana. However, there are eight differences: 1) age, 2) height, 3) clan, 4) duration of fasting, 5) bodily rays, 6) vehicles used in renunciation, 7) the Bodhi Tree under which they were enlightened, and 8) in the size of the seat upon which the Buddha sat.

The differences are illustrated by comparing the most familiar of the early Buddhas, Dipankara, with the last four. Dipankara and Kakusandha practiced abstinence or *dikkarakacariya* for ten months, Kassapa for seven days, Konagamana for six months, and Buddha Gotama for six years. Dipankara and Konagamana departed their privileged existence upon an elephant; Kakusanda rode a chariot pulled by thoroughbreds; Kassapa departed in a flying palace; and the Buddha Gotama rode upon a horse. Upon Kassapa's departure, his wife, her attendants, and many of Kassapa's male attendants accompanied the Bodhisattva. The men renounced with world, and the women retreated some distance from Kassapa and lived in temporary shelters. Dipankara and Kassapa were enlightened under a *Ficus obtusifolius* (Pali *nigrodha*) tree; Kakusandha under an *Acacia sirissa* (Pali *sirisa*) tree; Konagamana under a *Ficus indica* (Pali *udumbara*) tree. The last three – Kakusandha, Konagamana and Kassapa – came from Brahmin clans whereas all the previous Buddhas had come from aristocratic clans.

The Kakusandha Buddha was blessed with a clear and full voice and disciples with unblemished morality. Konagamana taught of the supermandane *Dhamma* and his disciples could exercise supernatural powers. Kassapa Buddha and his Buddhas taught the Gem of the *Dhamma*, embodying unmeasurable qualities. While the textual basis for their differences is not apparent in their images, the existence of their varied lives prompts the tellings of their stories, an essential aspect of spreading the teachings of the *Dhamma*.

On the evenings of the Festival of Lights the Shwedagon is transformed by thousands of candles. Here, nuns make an offering and pay homage.

Sacred Relics: a Comparison with Cambodia

The Shwedagon enshrines eight Sacred Hairs of the Buddha Gotama but also the relics of the three previous Buddhas of our era. It stands apart from all the other pagodas of Myanmar in this quantity of sacred relics. Cambodia, for example, has no equivalent shrine. There are other important differences between Buddhism in these two countries which highlight the uniqueness of the Myanmar tradition.

From the earliest adoption of Indic practices in Myanmar, perhaps 300 years after the death of the Buddha Gotama, the religion has been characterised by a flexibility and syncretism. Images and artefacts of Mahayana and Hindu sects have been recovered from Pyu sites dating to the pre-Pagan era before the 9th century. This is also the case for the range of early Indic-derived remains of Cambodia. While a range of rituals and beliefs flourished in both countries during the subsequent centuries, Hinduism and, briefly, Mahayana Buddhism, dominated Cambodian belief from about the 7th-13th century. During this time, Theravadan practice formed the core of the ancient cities of central and southern Myanmar. Cambodia (and Thailand) adopted Theravada Buddhism as the national religion and the basis of the state only from the 14th century. In Myanmar, Theravada continued without interruption after Pagan. It remains the principal religion of the nation today. In Cambodia, the devastation of the Pol Pot regime suppressed and virtually destroyed Buddhist and animistic practice.

The current revival of both in Cambodia provides an interesting comparison to Myanmar. Some customs in Cambodia are quite different. For example, the four Buddhas of our era are associated with an animal vehicle: the cock for Kakusandha, the serpent or *naga* for Konagamana, the tortoise for Kassapa, and the buffalo for Gotama. The relationship between veneration of spirits and that of the Buddha is in a process of change, for only a few elder persons remain alive who recall the practices of the earlier part of this century. The comparison is revealing in highlighting the relative wealth and elaboration of current practice in Myanmar. This benefits from a continuity of the religion and an absence of Cambodia's tragic genocide. The rate of religious innovation has accelerated in Myanmar in the last ten years to a degree yet to be seen in Cambodia.

During the dry season, pagodas all over the country are repaired. The upper portion of the Naung Daw Gyi Stupa [31] is swathed in matting to protect the superstructure during regilding.

Sacred Shrines: Kyaiktyo Pagoda

One example of current popular belief in Myanmar involves the Kyaiktyo pagoda, south of Yangon. It is often compared to the Shwedagon in its sacredness. An enormous rock, gilded and topped with a golden *stupa*, it perches impossibly on the edge of a precipice. In shape, despite the small *stupa* on the top of the boulder, the Kyaiktyo would seem an odd comparison for the Shwedagon. Yet in the shops around the platform of the Shwedagon, the story of the Kyaiktyo is related, and images abound showing the Shwedagon to the right and Kyaiktyo to the left. There are many versions of the Kyaiktyo story.

One involves a female with occult powers, daughter of a *weiza* and a female serpent known as Shwe Nan Kyin. A Karen or Kayin family raised her, and she eventually married. At the same time there was a hermit living in the forest, a prince who had renounced his throne in favour of his father, known a the 'King who is giver of good things' or Thupeyna Min. When the husband learned of his wife's supernatural powers, he left, and she disappeared. Two giant eggs were left behind, from which were born human children. They were raised by an elderly couple in the forest, and received teaching from the hermit prince. During his life in the forest, the hermit guarded a hair of the Buddha within a turban on his head. This had been brought to the hermit by another hermit, Theiktha, a disciple of the Buddha Gotama in the time after he had attained Nirvana.

Eventually the courtiers of the palace sought out the hermit prince, for the king had died and the throne was empty. The young man took the throne. At his death, he asked for a shrine to be built in his likeness, with the rock being his head and the *stupa* at the summit enshrining the hair of the Buddha, which he had guarded throughout his life. This rendition of the story is close to that depicted in the painted reliefs of Daw Pwint's Hall [8], on the southwest side of the platform, next to the Arakanese or Rakhine Hall.

Other versions of the story are quite different, with Shwe Nan Kyin marrying the King of Thaton, south of Yangon. In these the rock is her body which proved impossible to cremate. She had neglected to carry out a traditional Karen rite when she married. When she became pregnant, she tried to make amends but the spirits declined, sending a tiger to devour her. She died, declaring that she should stay there forever. A third version is a simplified rendition of the first, where a hermit living in the forest wishes for a shrine built resembling his head, and the shrine of the Sacred Hair. Thagyarmin or Sakka, Lord of the Nats or spirits, is asked to find a stone great enough, and places it upon the precipice.

Images of the Shwedagon and Kyaiktyo abound. They are sold not only as posters such as this one, but are seen on protective pendants with one shrine on each side. In Myanmar script, the first letter of Shwedagon is the same as the last letter of Kyaiktyo, while the letter beginning the last syllable of Shwedagon is the same as the first letter of Kyaiktyo. Their juxtaposition recalls this auspicious pairing, adding another layer of meaning to images of two of Myanmar's most sacred shrines.

During festivals, and indeed throughout the year, eminent *sayadaws* offer sermons to the assembled faithful.

Deciding which story is 'correct' is less important than the fact that it may be told in many different ways, the creation of a sacred temple which houses a Hair of the Buddha Gotama. All date Kyaiktyo after the lifetime of the Buddha, when he had attained Nirvana, with the Hair being brought to Myanmar by Thagyarmin. The link between the Shwedagon and Kyaityo may be this common housing of a Hair of the Lord Buddha, the Shwedagon dating to the time of the Buddha and the Kyaiktyo somewhat later.

Some people give a more magical explanation for the proliferation of images of Kyaiktyo at the Shwedagon, and the popularity of cards bearing pictures of both temples. In Myanmar writing the words 'Shwedagon Kyaityo' is a palindrome, as in the English phrase 'rats live on no evil star'. These form an *in-gwet* or magic diagram, protecting the bearer against evil.

Runes and Magic Diagrams

The place of runes, formulations of numbers and letters, exists in connection with innumerable aspects of images and pagodas in Myanmar. There is a clear link between the abundance of numerological calculations and the importance of astrology, seen in the planetary posts of the Shwedagon. Veneration at one's planetary post is widely accepted, whether for personal reasons or as a *yadaya*, an act to fulfill a donation formulated by an astrologer to grant a wish or solve a problem. The belief in the Shwedagon-Kyaiktyo diagram is a more popular one. A packet of plastic coated cards, the size of a calling card, may be carried in a man's shirt-pocket over his heart, with images of Bo Min Kaung, Shin Thiwali, and the Shwedagon-Kyaiktyo pagodas. Larger pictures or images may be placed on, or under, household shrines. Level of education has little bearing on those who might carry or use these images. Some educated persons are quick to deny 'belief', while others eloquently describe their faith.

None of these practices are part of canonical Buddhism as officially promulgated by the *Sangha*. However, there is a vast and complex body of meanings, pairings and diagrams that emanate from the shrines and images of the Shwedagon. To deny their existence, and also to neglect the sophistication of their use by a large percentage of those who come to the Shwedagon, gives an incomplete portrait of the place of the pagoda in contemporary belief.

Zawgyis and *Weizas*: Shin Ajagona, Bo Bo Aung and Bo Min Kaung

The word alchemist or *zawgyi* refers to the ability to change base metal into gold, a magic feat linked to wealth and longevity. A shrine on the north side of the Shwedagon platform, attached to the south side of the Naung Daw Gyi stupa, is dedicated to the *zawgyi* Shin Ajagona. His legend, from the Pagan era, recounts attempts to turn base metal into gold. The formula he used was incorrect, specifying pure gold, and he spent all his money on purchasing the precious metal. Having failed to perform for the king, he was punished, his eyes removed. Cast into a pile of faeces they gave off a shower of sparks.

Eventually, Shin Ajagona succeeded in using his philosopher's stone to produce pure gold when he touched the stone to base metal. Returned to royal favour, Shin Ajagona sent for two eyes to replace those removed by the king. The first two that his servants found were of unequal size, one from a goat, the other from a bull. His image, in the far corner of the shrine depicts him with one large and one small eye.

In addition to *zawgyis*, other associated powers can be acquired which bring greater wisdom and chances of true wealth in the form of immortality. Such men are called *weizas*, a higher level of the occult arts and being than *zawgyis*. A shrine on the north side of the Shwedagon platform is called the Weiza Tazaung, or Hall of the Weizas. Among the many figures paying homage to the central image of the Buddha are Thagyarmin, Lord of the Nats; Thurathati, guardian of wisdom; the hermit of Kyaiktyo; and the two most prevalent *weizas* at the Shwedagon, Bo Bo Aung and Bo Min Kaung. These last two achieved their powers through their ability to read runes or magic diagrams and through meditation, respectively.

Bo Min Kaung is the more recent of the two, and perhaps currently most popular for that reason. His modern existence is illustrated in his preference for cigarettes, rather than the more old-fashioned betel offerings given to Bo Bo Aung. Images of Bo Min Kaung, who lived some 100 years ago, are found within many of the shrines of the Shwedagon. A larger statue is found in the northeast sector of the pagoda platform, covered in gold leaf, and popularly venerated with gifts of *tha-bye* or Eugenia leaves, and cigarettes. Most images of Bo Min Kaung, however, are small, and sit amongst many others in front of images of the Buddha. He generally sits cross-legged, although he may be standing, holding his staff. Sometimes his hair is shaved, commemorating his period of meditation or it may be long, almost reaching his shoulders. He wears a *longyi*, or man's loose lower garment, often in a checked pattern, and a short Shan-style jacket.

Each image of the Buddha is unique. Offerings are constantly renewed such as the fresh and bright umbrellas donated here.

Images do not stand in isolation but, as seen here, are surrounded by smaller ones, with donatory boxes for re-gilding and adorning the images. A Myanmar friend once said that just as a woman is more beautiful adorned with jewels, naturally an image of the Lord Buddha is made beautiful with gold, jewels, and finely woven fabrics.

Unlike the aged territorial guardian Bo Bo Gyi, the lines on his face are not deep, but neither is he a young man. His expression is intense, and he leans forward in a meditation pose. Although Bo Min Kaung is not exclusively associated with the Shwedagon, his links to the shrine and to Yangon are strong. There is no precise date for his birth, although it is generally placed within the last 100 years. He is seen as combining self-discipline and meditation to gain his powers. Some believe he has the ability to duplicate himself. He may thus still be seen, anywhere, or everywhere.

More often than not, an image of Bo Min Kaung appears alongside an image of Bo Bo Aung. His appearance and history are quite different from Bo Min Kaung, although he shares with him the triumph of morality over power through pacific means. As with Bo Min Kaung there is not a precise date for his birth, but it is generally associated with the reign of 18th century King Bowdawpaya.

Images of Bo Bo Aung may be seated or standing. He is dressed in a loose white robe, not the garment of a monk, not an *arahat*, but a holy lay man who has gained some of the Perfections taught by the Lord Buddha. He often holds meditation beads, the 108 beads recalling the 108 marks of an auspicious man, like the marks on the footprint of the Buddha. Although Bo Bo Aung meditated, it is said he received his powers through his ability to read runes. His legend, placed some 500 years ago, begins with three friends who promised to remain loyal to each other forever. One was Bo Bo Aung. The second became a monk, and the third became king. During his reign, the king began to see the powers of Bo Bo Aung as a threat, for he could not only read runes or magic diagrams, but also could change mercury and iron into gold.

Implicit in these powers was the ability to be alive at the coming of Ari Mettaya, the future Buddha, and like all those alive at this time, become immortal. Eventually the king had Bo Bo Aung imprisoned, and tried unsuccessfully to kill him. Bo Bo Aung defeated all attempts to end his life, using again and again his powers achieved through reading of the runes or magic diagrams. He defied the king to erase even a letter which he wrote, and chose the letter *wa* which is written as a circle in Myanmar script. The choice was a careful one, for the circle carries the power to write all the other letters of the Myanmar alphabet.

One shrine attributed to Bo Bo Aung is on the northeast of the platform, just south of the Shin Ajagona Pavilion [30]. Maintained by the Sasana Dhamma Rakita Athin or Association, it is said to have an underground passageway to the Hair Washing Well. Its principal image sits within a cyst-like cell deep inside the *stupa*. Another shrine, on the west side of the Shwedagon, is more commonly attributed to Bo Bo Aung. It said to have been donated by him some 500 years ago. The shrine is small, but extremely popular. An equally venerated pavilion sits directly behind the Bo Bo Aung shrine, to the south, and contains an image donated by the Mon King Dhammaceti. Adjoining these two shrines is the meditation cave of Bo Min Kaung. Bo Bo Aung is said by some to live today in the forest outside Pye (Prome), north of Yangon.

He is also associated with the Ruby-Eyed or Mya Shin Buddha in a niche on the upper platform, on the south side. Historically this image was placed in a shrine built to cover a tunnel carved into the pagoda by the British in the mid-19th century. However, some believe that Bo Bo Aung placed a poem underneath the image. It describes his powers of creation from the size of a sesamun seed to the breadth of the universe, and the hope for the one that recites the prayer that all this power may come to me. Others say that the Ruby-Eyed image is that of Ari Mettaya, the Buddha to come.

Thus aspects of the lives of both Bo Bo Aung and Bo Min Kaung are directly linked to the Shwedagon. In addition, the two stories are parallel in placing an individual at the Shwedagon, and in using his life to demonstrate that self-discipline, strength and power of meditation are a means of achieving immortality. All these elements explain the presence of single images of either figure of a pair, with Bo Bo Aung to the right of the Buddha and Bo Min Kaung to the Buddha's left at shrines throughout the Shwedagon.

A number of images are protected by glass or grills. Nevertheless they too receive offerings, here pink roses.

A monk reciting prayers into a microphone is almost hidden by the shrine's offerings, from fresh flowers to bright metallic streamers.

A shop specialising in papier mache, including the ever-popular pairs of owls, one male, the other female.

Page 125
Inside the many pavilions of the Shwedagon, images surround and protect the devotee, while a craftsman repaints one of the Buddha images.

Visitors to the Shwedagon are free to do whatever they choose to gain peace of mind. The man here reads a text written out on the back of an old calendar.

Shin or *Arahat*: the Holy Monks Shin Thiwali and Upako

Another pair of images often seen flanking the Lord Buddha is that of Shin Thiwali and Shin Upako. The word *shin* roughly translates as holy monk, or *arahat*. The same word is part of the novitiation ceremony of young boys into the monkhood, the Shin-byu ceremony.

Both were monks, with Shin Thiwali living in the time of the Buddha Gotama and Shin Upako living after the Buddha's lifetime. Shin Thiwali is usually standing, holding his staff and his fan, head shaven, and wearing the robe of a monk. Popular cards of him show guardians or *devas* offering flowers, and creatures of the forest such as the monkey, offering honey. Shin Thiwali was well-known in the time of the Buddha Gotama for his kind and generous nature, one that reached back through many previous lives. As a result, many people offered him gifts, and he became quite rich. The Buddha delivered a sermon to his disciples cautioning them against jealousy, reminding his pupils that the gifts showered upon Shin Thiwali were the result of his accrued merits. Today he is favoured both for his example of generosity and kindness and in hopes that his veneration will bring wealth to the donor.

Shin Upako lived after the time of the Buddha. He had gained great powers such as the ability to meditate floating on the sea, and the power to deter the rains from coming. During his meditation, the evil Mara had tested him by bringing endless rains, but Upako's goodness and generosity defeated his attempts. Today Shin Upako is usually depicted seated, holding his begging bowl and dressed the robes of a monk. He gazes upwards towards the sky, and is often placed in a small pavilion set within a shallow bowl of water in memory of his victory over Mara. His veneration is less tied to great wealth than hopes of success in all undertakings and power to defeat any obstacles.

The pair Shin Thiwali and Shin Upako share with Bo Bo Aung and Bo Min Kaung different lifetimes, with Shin Thiwali and Bo Bo Aung living long ago, and Shin Upako and Bo Min Kaung in the more recent past. They are also alike as examples of meditation and the rewards to be gained in this lifetime and the next.

Wish-granting Images and Festivals

All these types of images can be seen during a clockwise circumference or circumambulation of nine wish-granting places or *ah-pweh*. Of these places, five are images of the Buddha. One is a pavilion linked to the founding of the Shwedagon, and three are associated with occult figures. A visit to any one of these may grant present or future wishes, although some feel a complete circuit is needed to ensure success.

The first is the Mya Shin or Ruby-eyed shrine, on the upper platform on the east side [46]. Some devotees link this image to the *weiza*, Bo Bo Aung. Others feel he represents the future Buddha, Ari Mettaya. The second is a group of white *stupas* known as Ah-pweh Weiza Zawgyi, on the southwest of the platform [7]. On the upper part are a number of *zawgyis* and *weizas* who came for meditation at midnight on the full moon of Waso (July-August). The third is located north of Singu's bell, a shrine known as Hman Thu Yin, whose Wonder Working Image is said to have been donated by the Mon Hanthawaddy ruler Shin Saw Bu in the 15th century [19]. Hanthwaddy is the historical name for the Mon capital at Pegu (Bago), east of Yangon. Although offerings are given by both men and women to the shrine, it is especially favoured by women, for Shin Saw Bu was not only one of the most generous benefactors to the Shwedagon, but also a Queen. Four flowering trees grow around Shin Saw Bu's shrine. The fourth wish-granting place is the Hair Washing Well, forming a key part of the founding legends of the pagoda [26]. The fifth is on the east perimeter of the platform, a pavilion known as Shin Ma Ti, in honour of the donor of the central image. The sixth place is the shrine of the alchemist of the Pagan era, Shin Ajagona or Izzagona [30]. The seventh is the Bo Bo Aung shrine on the east of the platform [35]. Some pilgrims cite the Bo Bo Aung shrine on the north of the platform as well. The eighth is a large image in the wish-granting or *varada* posture, on the south side of the Eastern Tazaung dedicated to the first Buddha of our *kappa*, Kakusandha [38]. The ninth place is the Mercury planetary shrine or Pa Da Shin Hpaya, south of east staircase on the perimeter of the platform.

The purpose and ritual of pilgrims to the Shwedagon varies tremendously. For some the planetary posts are key, for others worship of a single image or a prescribed path including images and shrines. While these are individual acts of devotion and merit-making there are also innumerable communal occasions at the Shwedagon. The faces of the four main images in the cardinal Devotional Halls are washed on each Full Moon day. Festivals marking the Full Moon day of each month are one part of the cycle of celebrations at the pagoda.

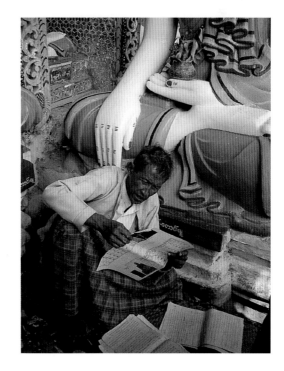

A *manuthiha* and planetary post form part of the architecture on this corner of the platform.

The Tabaung festival is held in February-March to celebrate the deposit of the Hair Relics, for they were first enshrined on the Full Moon Day of Tabaung, a Wednesday. The Buddha gained enlightenment on a Wednesday, the Full Moon Day of Kason (May) and gave His Hair Relics to the two merchant brothers from Myanmar on the fifth waxing day of the moon of Waso (July), also a Wednesday. April brings Thin-gyan or the Water Festival, marking the New Year. The beginning of the rainy seasonal is a time when monks retreat to their monasteries, and is marked by the offering of *kathein* or robes for the monks. Thadingyut in October is the festival of lights. In the evenings during the Thadingyut festival the platform glows with candlelight, and crowds of pilgrims circle the pagoda. The festival marks the end of the rains, and the return of the Buddha Gotama to earth from heaven, where He had journeyed after His enlightenment to preach to His mother. Marriages are generally banned during this period of the retreat and rains, from July to October.

At the end of the period of retreat, the end of the rains, monks are again offered robes in the Tazaung-daing or Kathein festival in October-November. This is also the occasion of the annual Robe Weaving Competition. Teams of women from all regions of the county compete in an all-night weaving marathon to produce the finest robes for the pagoda's images of the Buddha. The robes are carefully judged, and then are used to clothe selected images. The Kason festival is held in May, with a ceremony at the large Banyan tree [41]. The tree, grown from a seed of the Bo tree at Bodhgaya, is ceremonially watered at daybreak under the auspices of the Mahabodhi Society founded in the 1920s. This marks the anniversary of the birth of the Buddha Gotama, his attainment of Buddhahood, and his attainment of Nirvana.

Evening devotions during the Festival of Lights include not only monks and nuns, but people from every walk of life.

A formal portrait to record the young boys' Shin-byu Ceremony and the Ear-boring Ceremony for the young girls.

Buddha images are sometimes carried in procession around the platform during certain festivals.

Devotees drink holy water during the Tabaung Festival.
The *stupa* encases a relic. This may be an image of the Buddha or one of the many other types of sacred reminders of the Buddha Gotama or previous Buddhas.

Htis or umbrellas adorn the pinnacles of *stupas* crowning some of the small shrines on the pagoda platform. The distinctive Mahabodhi Stupa may be seen in the background.

Heavy monsoon rains do not deter devotees from their visits.

Pyat-that and *Stupas*

The pattern of ritual is not predetermined on a visit to the Shwedagon. Any object or act may offer a focus. There is choice in the offerings – flowers, umbrellas, incense, candles – and freedom in where to place them. Each of the pavilions on the platform is unique in its architecture and the images within. The replica of the Mahabodhi temple in Benares rises in the typical *sikhara* of northern India. Many shrines are topped with a small *stupa*, mirroring the form of the main pagoda. These rounded spires are complemented by the tiered roof of the *pyat-that*, traditionally used to mark both royal and religious architecture.

The Buddha-to-be is seen seated in a position of royal ease before *pyat-thats* of five, seven and nine tiers on plaques inside the 11th century Ananda temple at Pagan. These recall palaces built for Prince Siddartha before his abdication of royal power to become the Enlightened One, the Buddha Gotama. The *pyat-that* frames a royal figure within a shrine dedicated to the four Buddhas of our era. A statue of King Kyanzittha, who built the temple, is found at the centre of the pagoda. The *pyat-that* is used at the Ananda in both royal and religious contexts. In the use of the *pyat-that*, and in many other historical, architectural and ritual aspects, religious merit and royal power are also joined at the Shwedagon. Royal donations to the Shwedagon, for instance, have traditionally signalled sovereignty over the Delta area.

The tiered roofs of the Shwedagon are made from many different materials, including wood, tin, and concrete. The wood-carving of Myanmar is justly famous, in particular the graceful forms of the *pyat-that*, in continuous use in palace and monastery architecture for the last thousand years. Remnants of old wood-carving are found at various places on the platform [34]. New wood-carving is sharp; its chiseled angles providing bright spots to reflect light and shine like mirrors. Likewise, the facets of metal *pyat-that* catch the light. Myanmar royal and religious architecture has always been marked by this combination of traditional and modern methods of constructions. Forms may be old, but created in new materials.

The round *stupas* at the Shwedagon are also constantly repaired, painted white, yellow or gold. Some are gilded with gold leaf. *Stupas* vary from the mass of the central *stupa* to those that crown many of the small shrines on the pagoda platform. The form of the *stupa* is thought to have come from burial mounds pre-dating the birth of the Buddha Gotama in the sixth century BC. After His attainment of Nirvana or enlightenment, the disciples of the Buddha distributed his relics, enshrining them in *stupas*.

At the Shwedagon, every *stupa* marks a relic. In the case of the central *stupa* these are said to be relics not only of the Buddha Gotama but the four previous Buddhas of our era. Many other *stupas* crown a simple cell sheltering an image of the Buddha. Often the symbolism of the *stupa* is seen to reiterate that of the image. While the *pyat-that* marks a sacred or royal place, the *stupa* and the image of the Buddha are close in both formal and cosmological significance. For example, the *stupa* is centred on an axis, just as the Buddha attained enlightenment while mediating under the shelter of and against the axis of the Bodhi tree. The sacred space of the *stupa* radiates from the axis mundi, and the elements of the *stupa* both rise and expand. From the lower square terraces, the rounded form of the *anda* or bell, to the spire, the levels are likened to the stages towards enlightenment experienced by the Buddha.

The *pyat-that* and *stupas* shelter the images of the Buddha Gotama, scenes from his life, and his 550 previous lives, the *jatakas*. There are images of the four Buddhas of our era: Kakusandha, Konagamana, Kassapa, and Gotama. Other images are of the 28 Buddhas. There are also images of occult masters, spirit and guardian figures, mythical animals, and animals associated with the planetary posts. Some figures are particularly venerated, although there is no common explanation for the admiration of particular shrines. At the Fertility Shrine [43] a guardian or *deva* carries a small child. The shrine is one of the many around the base of the pagoda. It also shelters an image of the Buddha, but the infant in the arms of a *deva* on one side of the entry makes it popular with woman wishing to bear a child.

The Wonder Working Image [19] has long been known to grant miracles, and many offerings of gold leaf have made the image thick with gold. The image in the Shrine of the Sun and Moon has recently become popular [5]. Two large gold medallions form an arch over its entry. They display a peacock and a rabbit, symbols of the Sun and Moon. On the southeast of the platform is a prayer post or *dagun-daing* surmounted by the figure of an *arahat* [40]. There are various explanations for this image. Some say the monk incurred the Buddha's displeasure, displaying supernatural powers by flying through the air in order to win a wager. Others cite it as a remembrance of legends of the origin of the prayer-post, topped with a begging bowl or *thabaeik*. According to legend, in the time of the Buddha, He placed a bowl at the summit of the pillar, an example of the difficulty of gaining merit. Any monk who could reach the bowl would be blessed with abundant alms. None could reach it, but one monk with magical powers was able to fly to the top and retrieved the bowl.

In the 1970s and 1980s the shrines surrounding the main *stupa* were painted red in comparison with the deep yellow of today.

The wet marble does not deter devotees from kneeling to pay hommage to the pagoda.

Donations may be money for upkeep of the pagoda, a shrine, or an image. They may be precious metals or gems, flowers, or water. Water offerings for Buddhas on planetary posts are said to give coolness to mind and body. They may be donatory bowls rotating on a plinth, waiting for coins to be thrown and wishes made, such as at the Hall of the Carousel where one may wish for good health or success in business by throwing money into a certain bowl [44]. Victory or *tha-bye* leaves from the Eugenia plant may be offered. Shawls may be given to the guardian spirit of the pagoda, the Bo-Bo-Gyi [7], standing to the left of an image of Sakka or Thagyarmin, Lord of the Spirits or Nats. Water may be poured over the image of the Buddha at one of the planetary shrines. The earth goddess, Wathondari, stored the accumulated merits of the Buddha, in her long hair. Just before his enlightenment, when the evil army of Mara attacked the Buddha, Wathondari washed the armies away by ringing out her long tresses in testimony to the vast merit of the Buddha.

The Main Stupa

The 99 metre-high *stupa* of the Shwedagon has been enlarged many times over the centuries. The present structure encases earlier *stupas*, but stands independent of them. It dates to the 1770s.

The shape of the *stupa* as a bell or bowl shape is an ancient architectural form for a relic chamber which may be traced back to the Great Stupa at Sanchi in Madhya Pradesh, one of 84,000 allegedly built by Asoka, the first Buddhist ruler, in the 3rd century BC. The huge hemispherical dome is reminiscent of a relic mound and must have provided the model for many subsequent *stupas*. Chinese literary sources translated from Indian 7th century texts also discuss the origin of the *stupa* as being derived from the three robes of the Buddha folded and stacked with an inverted alms bowl and staff on top. However it is in Sri Lanka that the classic bell-shape was developed, a form which is found in Myanmar and Thailand. The Thuparama was constructed by King Devanampiyatissa in the 3rd century BC and rebuilt in the 5th and 7th centuries AD. Its most striking characteristic in comparison with Sanchi is that the flat terrace has now been developed into a spire. In Myanmar the *stupa* which is the most important precursor to the Shwedagon is the Shwezigon pagoda at Bagan, begun by Anawratha (r.1044-77) and completed by Kyanzittha (1084-1113). A comparison between the two, highlights the elegance of the Shwedagon. The divisions between the various parts has been smoothed out and the banana bud has been elongated and given greater prominence.

Its perimeter is huge, 443 metres set on the level platform, some 274 by 213 metres. The base is low, only 0.69 metres high, and hidden behind a multitude of shrines. The four large Devotional Halls or *Tazaung* mark the centre of each face. Between these are 64 single-cell shrines, *zeidi-yan*, painted bright yellow, each crowned with a small golden *stupa*. In the 1970s they were painted red. They were not always there, for the shrines are absent in photographs of the 1890s. By 1906, however, the small cells ring the base of the *stupa*. The shrines and the spaces between are filled with figures. There are images of the Buddha everywhere, inside and outside shrines and seated in front of planetary posts.

There are also inhabitants of the six lower levels of heaven; from guardian *devas* to inferior and superior ogres, *gonban* and *yakha bilus*. Other images are alchemists, *zawgyi*. There are mythical lions, *chinthe*. Four large double lion body figures, with the face of a man, *manuthiha* sit behind some of the planetary shrines. The *manuthiha* is said to have come from the Mon peoples

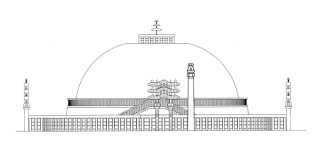

Great Stupa, Sanchi, Madhya Pradesh, India.

Thuparama Pagoda, Anuradhapura, Sri Lanka.

Shwezigon Pagoda, Bagan.

of Myanmar. The human-faced double lion-bodied *manuthiha* recall the supernatural creature created to frighten an ogress and ogre who had been terrorizing the countryside by eating small children. Large *manuthiha* have marked the lower edges of the central *stupa* since early in this century.

Above the base is the plinth, 6.5 metres high and 6 metres wide. Little is seen of the plinth from the platform. However, sixty-four *stupas* are set around its edge. These form a tier behind the shrines around the base. Behind the four Devotional Hall are larger structures, *stupas* on the east and west and shrines on the north and south.

On an acroteria fixed to the plinth on the west are statues of Sakka or Thagyarmin and Mai Lamu [10]. Sakka and Mai Lamu are the legendary father and mother of King Okkalapa, ruler of Dagon in the time of the Buddha when His Sacred Hairs came to Shwedagon Hill. The Mai Lamu pagoda, in North Okkalapa, was built on the spot where Mai Lamu lived, at that time a forested area with wild animals. Mai Lamu was born from a fruit which the hermit, living in the forest, picked from a Lamu tree (*Sonneratia caseolaris*).

When Mai Lamu was grown Sakka transformed himself into a young man and married her. When he returned to heaven, Mai Lamu became ill with grief. Sakka then sent her a flask of holy water on the back of a dove. A hawk, Sakka's jealous queen, attacked the dove. Nonetheless, a few drops were saved. When these reached Mai Lamu she gave birth to a son, named Okkalapa, who grew up to found the kingdom of Dagon. There is a small statue of King Okkalapa, also on the main shrine, but north of the Kassapa Devotional Hall at the head of the western staircase.

There are three square terraces on the main *stupa*, *pyit-sayan*, rising 19 metres. The terrace corners are in the *kho-nan* style, with seven angles or folds of equal dimensions. The term literally means pigeon house of palace. Some say the design comes from the criss-crossed steps of a pigeon. Others relate the story of a notorious prince, who possessed a prize pigeon. The bird bore a grain in his beak each day to present to the king. One day, however, he quit the service of the king in favour of the prince. The king hit the bird with a stick; he became lame, and then died. Out of remorse, the king built a small house in his memory on top of the palace roof. *Kho-nan* angles became popular during the 17th century Nyaung-yan period, and are associated with Mon influence at the 15th century Hanthawaddy court at Pegu. Their incorporation into the base of the *stupa* may date to the offerings of Hanthwaddy's Queen Shin Saw Bu.

Above the three terraces are octagonal tiers, 8 metres high. The corners are also folded in the *kho-nan* style, although there are five rather than seven

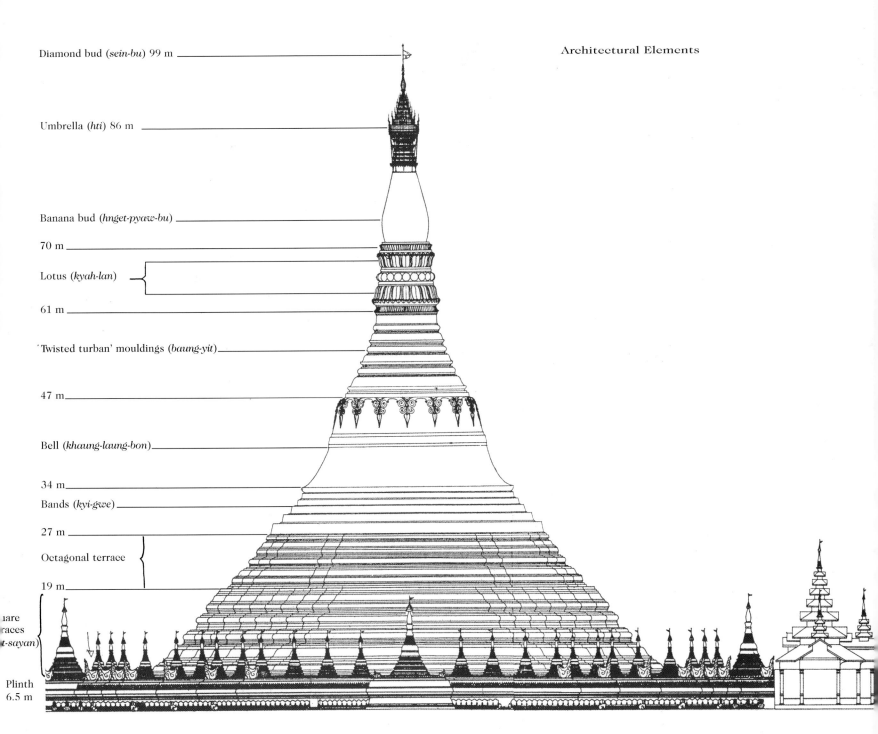

Architectural Elements

Diamond bud (*sein-bu*) 99 m

Umbrella (*hti*) 86 m

Banana bud (*hnget-pyaw-bu*)

70 m

Lotus (*kyah-lan*)

61 m

'Twisted turban' mouldings (*baung-yit*)

47 m

Bell (*khaung-laung-bon*)

34 m

Bands (*kyi-gwe*)

27 m

Octagonal terrace

19 m

Square
terraces
(*…-sayan*)

Plinth
6.5 m

133

The curve of the banana bud or *hnget-pyaw-bu* contrasts to the sharp and light-catching corners of the *pyat-that* tiers.

angles. The *kho-nan* corners add a strong vertical element, leading the eye up to the curve of the bands and the bell. The five round bands, *kyi-gwe*, are slightly terraced with flat faces. They are plain today but were more elaborately decorated in earlier periods. Rising some 7 metres, the bands are a final transition to the smoothness of the bell.

The bell, *khaung-laung-bon* or inverted begging bowl, *tha-beik*, signifies a higher level of attainment than the lower terraces. It is curved rather than hemispherical. A band circles its midpoint. The shoulder of the bell is decorated with sixteen floral motifs, *pan-swe*. The bell is topped with rings called the 'twisted turban', *baung-yit*. Above the rings is the lotus, *kyah-lan*, 9 metres high. The nineteen petals of the flower, *kyah-yin* and *kyah-hmauk* are seen above and below a ring of nineteen inverted begging bowls, forming rounded bosses. The main petals are edged with smaller petals. From the lotus emerges the banana bud, *hnget-pyaw-bu*. Its curves echo the bell below. Some say the form comes from the shape formed by two hands placed together in prayer. The bud is more than 16 metres, a necessary height given its position on the upper part of the *stupa*; all elements are proportioned for viewing from the platform. It is inlaid with gold plates, texturing its surface.

Two late nineteenth century views from opposite sides of the *stupa*
show varying states of decoration and repair.

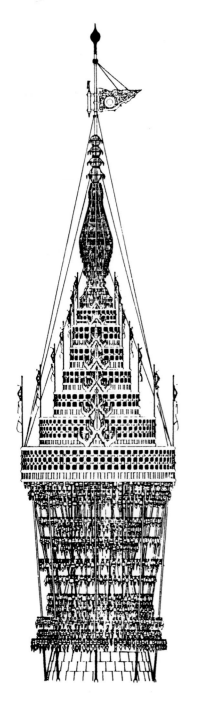

The *hti* caps the *hnget-pyaw-bu*. Below are the flowers and petals of the lotus, separated by a ring of inverted begging bowls, *kaung-laung-bon*.

The upper part of the main *stupa* is encased in scaffolding. Pulleys and a small trolley ferry materials up to the workers.

Each year different sections of the *stupa* are regilded.
The scaffolding allows labourers to ascend the pagoda;
the matting shelters the lower terraces from the sun.

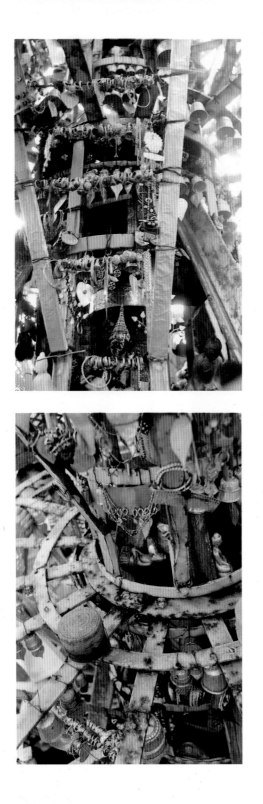

In 1900, a decision was made by the Pagoda Trustees to put one-foot square plates on the surface of the bud. These have been repaired and replaced over the years. By 1956, there were 9,272 plates, valued at some 12,800,000 *kyat*. The gold plates are fixed with screws to copper bands. This strengthens the upper parts of the *stupa* allowing it to carry the weight of the umbrella or *hti*. Every four years the pagoda is re-gilded on all the lower parts of the *stupa*. The re-gilding takes about 100 days, during which time it is encased in bamboo scaffolding and covered in matting. Before the new gold is applied the surface is scrubbed, and the gold dust gathered. During the dry season months not only the main shrine but many of the smaller pavilions may be renewed. Old photographs of both the main *stupa* and the Naung Daw Gyi *stupa* show this practice has long been customary. An annotation on a picture from 1855 notes that the gilding cost £15,000.

The *hti* is fixed to a brass capital at the top of the bud supported by wires, struts, rings and t-sections. The vane and orb, *sein-bu*, are held up by a centre shaft. The vane is referred to as *hhnget-mana* or *nget-myet-na*. The first, *hhnget-mana* means a place where a bird will not alight, which is correct. The second term, *nget-myet-na*, instead refers to a royal bird that has alighted. The *hti*, over 5 metres high, has seven iron tiers plated with gold. The tiers are inlaid with diamonds, rubies, emeralds and other gems. The main steel shaft, made of steel and covered in gold foil, rises above the *hti*. It carries an iron cone-shaped framework, *sattha-hpu*. The word *sattha* refers to the bud of a plant before it begins to flower, when it carries a sweet but pungent smell. The word *hpu* is the bud of the plant whereas *bu*, seen in *sein-bu* or diamond bud, is a less botanical description of a bud-like form.

Hanging from the rungs of the cone are gifts of jewelry and gold and silver bells. Four angled spheres, *zoon*, are above the cone, also hung with bells and jewels. Next is the vane, decorated with more than 1,100 diamonds, equaling 278 carats, and more than 1,300 rubies, sapphires and other gems. Its triangular surface is covered with gold and silver plates. At the very top is the orb, a ten-inch sphere, signifying Nirvana. Made of gold, it is decorated with gems: 4,351 diamonds weighing 1800 carats and 93 other stones. On the tip is a 76-carat diamond.

The immense superstructure of the *hti* requires a complex and massive inner framework to support its weight. The many gold bells, chains, precious stones, golden Buddha images and other items of personal jewellery donated over the centuries are attached to every part of the interior structure.

Below the orb the supporting rod is encased in a gold sleeve embossed with Buddha images.

The bejewelled and encrusted orb, the 76-carat diamond, the vane and a few of the many images donated to the upper portion of the stupa.

One of a number of images with wish-granting stones left for the devotee to use if he or she chooses. Wishes may range from success in exams to the blessing of a child. Prayer follows a first lifting of the stone. If it feels lights after devotions and offerings, the wish may be granted.

The Founding of the Pagoda

A well on the north of the main *stupa* marks the place where the Hair Relics of the Buddha were washed. The Shrine of the Hair Relics [26] combines brilliant green and white mosaic glasswork, on a pavilion erected over the well shaft. The pavilion shelters a brick-tiered shrine built in 1879, over the well, San-daw-dwin, in which the eight Sacred Hairs were washed before they were enshrined in the Naung Daw Gyi Stupa. The well reaches to the river, its water level rising and falling with the tide. The primitive well and the precisely cut and glittering glass of the shelter encapsulates the old and new of the Shwedagon.

The pavilion faces the Naung Daw Gyi Pagoda [31], the pagoda where the Hair Relics were first placed when the reached the Shwedagon. Literally, the 'elder royal large pagoda', this was built in the 16th century by King Bayinnaung. The first shrine to on this spot honouring the resting-place of the Sacred Hairs was said to have been built by King Okkalapa. The Naung Daw Gyi is traditionally cited as the model for the main *stupa*, and in photographs from 1900 it is remarkably similar to its form today. A straight line can be drawn from it to the Small Gilded Pagoda [28] and then to main *stupa*.

Next to the Small Gilded Pagoda is the 'Two-piece Pavilion' [29]. It contains three images of the Buddha, recalling the legend that King Okkalapa came to the Shwedagon Hill knowing that the relics of the three previous Buddhas of our era were enshrined. The king prayed that he might be allowed to place a relic of the Gotama Buddha. In a vision, the Buddha granted his request. Thus it was to him that the two brothers brought the Sacred Hair relics. Perhaps because of this association, the central image of the Buddha, more than two hundred years old, is a venerated 'prayer-granting' Buddha, Su-daung-byi.

Placed before the Su-daung-byi Buddha is a wish-granting stone. This is lifted prior to paying homage to the Buddha. The devotee then requests that the stone be made light if the wish is to be granted, and that it will remain heavy if the wish is to be denied. Some believe that a passageway behind the image leads to the relic chamber of the Sacred Hairs. A story related by Daw Khin Myo Chit, speaks of the well leading to a tunnel under the pagoda. At the end of the chamber there is said to be a large domed chamber, and at its centre, a deep hole whose water level changes with the tides of the river. The Hair Relics are said to be here, laid on top of precious gems within a jewel-studded golden barge in the form of the mythical Karaweik bird.

The Shwedagon Hill

The legend most commonly associated with the Shwedagon links it to the founding of the·Sule Pagoda to the south. In about 500 BC, the area was known as Okkala or Asitanjana. The word 'Okkala' or 'Ukkala' comes from 'Utkala', the Sanskrit transcription of Orissa in India. Although lacking firm archaeological evidence, many associate Utkala with a Buddhist or a Hindu colony, one of a number sited on elevated places around what became Yangon. Asitanjana is the name given to a settlement located northwest of the Shwedagon hill. Inscriptions also mention Ramannadesa, originally referring to the region between the Sittang and Salween Rivers.

The Shwedagon hill is most often called 'Singuttara'. Mon legends speak of three hills that bow down to Singuttara, so it is also called by a Sanskrit name, Trikumbha Nagara (kumbha being a 'conical object'). Other names for the hill are given by U Win Pe in his book on the Shwedagon:

"Singuttara Hill has seven names: Trihakumba, Sattabhummi, Dhannavati, Pokkaharavati, Bhuridatta, Siharaja, and Singuttara. It is called Trihakumba because three hilltops, the end of the Himalayan Forest, appear to bow down to the hill. It is called Sattabhummi because it has seven kinds of earth: golden, silvery, red, white, black, sour, bitter. It is called Dhannavati because of the abundance of grain, of treasure, of branches, of flowers. It is called Pokkaharavati because of the encircling 99 hills adorn Singuttara Hill. It is called Bhuridatta because enemies cease their enmities on reaching it. It is called Siharaja because from far it looks like a graceful lion. It is called Singuttara because for many years a centipede seized and ate elephants, so that the heap of their tusks had the height of seven palm trees. The name is given after the centipede and the tusks."

In the 6th century BC, the Shwedagon Hill may have been one of the few habitable areas around Yangon. Both the Shwedagon and Sule pagodas rest on lateritic outcrops, with other smaller shrines found on the many small hills between these two landmarks. At that time, the area of present-day Yangon was probably swampy or seasonally flooded. This raises questions about legends naming not only Ukkala (Yangon), but also the two much lower areas of Kusima (Bassein) and Muttima (Martaban). Just east of the Shwedagon are the Royal Lakes, the Kandawgyi and Kandawgale. So although the Shwedagon was elevated, it was adjacent to a naturally inundated low spot, fed by tidal streams to the south and springs along a ridge between the lakes and the hill.

Aerial photograph taken for reconaissance purposes by the British Royal Airforce in October 1944.

The 15th century Kalyani inscriptions erected by King Dhammaceti.

Later inscriptions.

The 15th century Inscriptions

The first epigraphic evidence we have in Myanmar for the Shwedagon is found on the Kalyani inscriptions erected by King Dhammaceti in the 15th century. The writing is Mon, with Burmese commentary on the other face, engraved on three stone slabs, each nearly four metres high. Over time, the slabs became buried, but found by Forchammer in 1880. Biggs, fifteen years later, notes unearthing them from a rubbish heap and turning them over to the Shwedagon Trustees, who placed them in a shrine. The inscriptions speak of the Hair Relic Pagoda, the Kesa-dhatu-chetiya; they include the name Tambagutta, 'guarded by copper', possibly reference to the encasing of the Sacred Hairs within the hill. The hill is called it Dgun, a Mon word. This may have become Lagun, then Dagon, according to Singer. The inscriptions begin with an account of a mission of Burmese monks sent to Sri Lanka for re-ordination. Upon their return, Dhammaceti journeyed from Pegu to Yangon to meet the monks. The King presented the Shwedagon with a large bell and other offerings.

The inscriptions also relate the story of the two brothers credited with bringing the Hairs of the Buddha to the Shwedagon. Various other scriptures refer to the brothers, Taphussa and Bhallika, but without linking them to the Shwedagon. Many authors doubt that the brothers came from Myanmar as the name Okkala derives from Orissa in India. An earlier Sri Lankan chronicle contains a similar story of hair relics from Orissa, but enshrined in Sri Lanka, not Myanmar. King Dhammaceti's inscription, however, describes the story as it has become accepted within Myanmar traditional history.

The Merchant Brothers

Two Okkala merchants, brothers Taphussa and Bhallika, heard that there was famine to the west, so traveled to India with a boatload of rice, which they placed on 500 ox-carts. These form part of wood-carvings on the east stair of the pagoda. The mother of the brothers had died and become a spirit or *nat*. She urged them to seek out the newly enlightened Buddha. In some versions of the story, the carts were halted by the *nat* at the spot the Buddha was to be found. The brothers came upon the Buddha on His seventh day of meditation under the *linlun*, a sacred Bo tree (*Buchanania latifolia*). They offered him cakes of honey decorated with golden flowers. At the same time four *nats* appeared from the lowest *deva* world, ruled by the Kings of the four directions. The *nats* tried to give the Buddha four sapphire bowls but He turned these down in favour of four plain stone bowls, the colour of brown peas. The Buddha changed the four into one bowl, into which the Okkala merchants placed their offering. The Buddha ate the honey cakes, and then delivered a sermon.

Upon their departure the brothers requested a token of remembrance from the Buddha, who gave them eight Hairs from His head. Sakka, Lord of the Nats, and ruler of Tavatimsa heaven, made a tiered shrine or *pyat-that*, adorned with rubies. Inside he placed an emerald casket, into which the brothers put the Hairs. The Buddha told them that the three previous Buddhas of this era had left objects at Singuttara Hill. They were to enshrine the Hairs on this hill. During their return journey, Taphussa and Bhallika met with various misadventures. Two of the Hairs were taken, one by the king in Orissa and another by the king of the Nagas, who had heard that the Hairs glowed with rays of six different colours.

When they neared Okkala (Yangon), the two brothers rested at the Sule pagoda as they were unable to find Singuttara Hill. Learning this, Sakka had the *nat* Vissakamma clear the trees on the hill and level its top, making it visible to the brothers. This was accomplished in a night, leaving the surface as smooth as a drum.

To prepare for the relics, a chamber was dug, 21 metres in length, breadth and height. In this cave, the relics of the three preceding Buddhas of our era were found; the water-dipper of Kakussanda by the Sule *nat*; the staff of Kasha [Kassapa] by the Dekkhina *nat*; and the lower garment of Konagamana by the Yawhani *nat*. These were interred again, along with the Sacred Hairs brought by Taphussa and Bhallika. The cave was lined with six marble slabs of diamond, silver, pearl, gold, sapphire and ruby colour. The Hairs once again, miraculously, numbered eight. Five jars of gold were brought into the relic chamber, placed at the corners and in the centre. A jeweled flower was put on the centre jar, and on top of the flower was placed a golden ship, a miniature of the ship in which the Hairs had come. Images of Sakka, the brothers, and other *nats* were placed in the chamber. The casket with the relics of the previous Buddhas was placed in a chamber, marked with a series of pagodas, each enclosed within the other: gold, silver, tin, copper, lead, marble, and iron. A brick pagoda, some twenty-seven feet high, covered the smaller pagodas.

Elaborate and exquisitely executed woodwork around an entry includes the story of the legendary Merchant Brothers.

As is customarily said, the form of the Naung Daw Gyi on the northeast of the platform remains little changed, but the wooden *tazaung* to the right illustrates the constant renovation needed for the pavilions. Note also the absence of the small shrines that now ring the main *stupa*.

The same *pyat-that* form seen on the northeast part of the platform is repeated here on the southern entry.

The Pagoda and Royal Authority

Little is recorded about the Shwedagon between its founding and the 14th century. Legends relate that a line of 32 kings ruled Dagon after the relics were enshrined; the pagoda then fell into disrepair. Around the third century BC, two monks, Sona and Uttara, are traditionally credited with the introduction of Buddhism to Myanmar. They reportedly also brought King Asoka to the Shwedagon. He repaired the pagoda, and cleared it of trees. The fifth century Pyu King Duttabaung of Srikshetra at Prome tried to remove the Sacred Hairs but was turned back by a storm. He instead worshipped at the pagoda, leaving an umbrella or *hti* with an emerald handle and diamond leaves on the southeast corner of the platform. King Anawratha of Pagan donated gold and silver *hti* in the 11th century. Anawratha also built a shrine on the northeast corner of the Shwedagon platform. Both offerings are linked to his conquest of the city of Thaton in 1057. The association of Asoka, and then Anawratha, continued the tradition of King Okkalapa where authority over the region was marked by offerings to the Shwedagon.

Dagon was known as a Mon fishing village, some say from the 11th century, others from the 14th. From the 14th century onwards, donations to the Shwedagon reflected fluctuations in power between lower and upper Burma, between the Mon kings of Pegu and the Burmese kings of Ava. In the mid-14th century, the Mon King of Pegu carried out repairs, raising the height of the pagoda to 21 metres. His son took shelter in Dagon, although after becoming king in 1385, he appears to have neglected the pagoda. In 1427, King Byinnyayan repaired the umbrella or *hti*, reduced the height of the hill, re-terraced it, and began a new brick and mortar casing for the *stupa*. The *stupa* was rebuilt up to the bell section by his successor.

Queen Shin Saw Bu

The most important royal patron of the 15th century was Queen Shin Saw Bu. Between 1455-62, the Queen gave her weight in gold to gild the pagoda and erect a new *hti*. She was thus the first to gild the shrine. She also enlarged the pagoda, to 40 metres, and terraced the hill. The platform was paved with stones, with seven walls built around the platform. Slaves and land for the pagoda maintenance were also donated. Queen Shin Saw Bu founded a new town northwest of the pagoda, in the area now known as Myenigon. She donated large tracts of land to the pagoda. The Queen made many appointments, including companies of watchmen on each side of the pagoda, headmen for gold work, plaster work, wood carvers, lamplighters, a land measurer, astrologers – a total of 1,006 men. Remnants of the stockade around her palace may still be seen west of the pagoda, on the land between U Wisara and Pye Road. She lived there up until her death in 1472, and it is said that during her final illness she commanded that her bed be moved so that she could see the Shwedagon spire. Today, Queen Shin Saw Bu's shrine [19] is said to have an image donated by her, making it particularly popular with women.

King Dhammaceti

Work continued on the pagoda during the 15th century, under King Dhammaceti, Shin Saw Bu's successor. He donated gold four times his weight and that of his queen to gild the pagoda, although this was partly to compensate for a reduction in the lands Queen Shin Saw Bu had donated. Dhammaceti ordered one large and several smaller bells cast, and added 50,000 stones to the platform paving. He also erected the famous inscribed slabs recording the history of the pagoda. His largest bell contained nearly five tons of bronze. Some years later, in 1608, the Portuguese Philip de Brito y Nicote who ruled Syriam, across the river from Yangon, removed the bell, hoping to use the metal for cannons. The attempt failed, however, and the boat sank in the middle of the river. Dhammaceti is also said to have instituted the custom of annual royal gifts, declaring that every year at the end of Buddhist Lent twenty-five trees with offerings like trees in flower be donated to the pagoda.

There are different versions of the acts of Dhammaceti's successor, Byinnyayan. In one, the king repairs the *hti*, builds forty-eight pagodas on an enlarged base, and makes offerings in golden alms-bowls with golden litters every day. However, in the second, his reign is presented as troubled: there was famine; *nats* stood in the sky and abused him; the *hti* blew down. Frightened by these evil portents, the King held a great festival and repaired the *hti*. He was 48 years old, and so built 48 small pagodas to end the stream of difficulties. The contrast in these two versions serves as a reminder that all royal donations were prompted both by devotion and political motives.

A view from the upper terrace including the Naung Daw Gyi Stupa.

The sumptuous carving in this view appears to overwhelm the devotees, but meditating in such an environment must have been a profoundly moving experience.

Not all of the small *stupas* were able to be repaired each year, but works were always carried out on the main stupa.

Early European Accounts and 16th–19th century Royal Donations

Europeans visits begin with the 15th century account of the Italian di Conti. But it is not until the 1583 description of Gasparo Balbi, that Dagon is included. The account of the Englishman, Ralph Fitch, closely parallels that of Balbi. Both mention the Shwedagon. Balbi also describes the monasteries or *kyaungs*:

"We saw wooden houses gilded, and adorned with delicate gardens, after their custome, wherein the Talapoins, which are their Friers, dwell, and looke to the Pagod, or Varella of Dogon."

Fitch's description is altogether more fulsome:

"It is the fairest place, as I suppose, that is in the world; it standeth very high, and there are foure ways to it, which all along are set with Trees of fruits, insuch wise that a man may goe in the shade above two miles in length. And when their Feast day is, a man can hardly passe by water or by land for the great presse of people; for they come from all places of the Kingdome of Pegu thither at their Feast." (Win Pe 1972:22) [The feast is probably the annual Shwedagon festival held on the full moon day of Tabaung (February-March)].

Numerous royal donations are recorded in the 16th century. The first was in 1508, when the king repaired the *hti*. The others were in 1526 and 1564, after earthquakes. The Shwedagon continued to grow in importance as a symbol of political power. King Tabinshwehti (r.1531-50) occupied Dagon, claiming sovereignty by making offerings to the Shwedagon. He even donated his queen, redeeming her with 36 pounds of gold. In 1564, when King Bayinnaung's queen died, there was an eclipse of the sun and an earthquake during which the hair relics crumbled down. The pagoda was disassembled to the middle stage, then rebuilt. The king raised the crown, and donated a gilded *hti*.

The course of the Pegu River altered in the late 16th century, and although Pegu remained a commercial centre, Syriam and Dagon became more important as ports. Dagon also continued as a fishing port, with Balbi noting that the fishing nets were a hazard to visiting boats. From the mid-17th century both Syriam and Dagon or 'Dogon' regularly appear on European maps.

King Anaukpetlun took Syriam in 1613, executing de Brito and making offerings to the Shwedagon, including a bell to replace Dhammaceti's bell.

King Anaukpetlun also erected a new hti with two thousand rubies, two viss of gold, and two viss of diamonds. He offered gifts during the September-October festival of Thadingyut and the February-March festival of Tabaung. These included golden flowers, golden parched grain, golden candles and silver candles and annual donations of gold leaf for the pagoda.

The ceremony surrounding the annual royal offerings suggest that the cycle of festivals at the Shwedagon provided occasion not only for royal processions but performances and markets:

"When the royal offerings came to be presented to the Shwe Dagon Pagoda the men of the household and the clerks had to carry the golden branches and the silver branches, the elders and the salt boilers had to carry the golden candlesticks and the silver candlesticks, the sitkes had to bear the umbrellas the pennants and the rosaries. At the observance of the royal almsgiving the boxers had to perform for three full days; the toll collectors and writers of the festival and the toll collectors and writers of the boats had to give the letpet for the prizes, the advocates had to hold the prizes and distribute them."
(Win Pe 1972:23 from the History of Syriam).

The pagoda was damaged in earthquakes throughout the centuries. Many of these coincided with dire events, such as the 1664 Thai attack on the Delta. Damage from the 1664 earthquake is recorded in great detail, and included damage to the *hti* and the banana bud. Offerings to repair the damage included 1,800 gems for the *hti*, a three-day festival with two orchestras, ten dancers, and food offered to 240 monks,

King Alaungpaya occupied Dagon in 1755, building a stockade the next year, and renaming the site Yangon ('end of strife'). The King destroyed Syriam, across the river, in 1756, adding to the growing importance of Yangon. Europeans noted that the area west of the Shwedagon, to the Rangoon River, was covered in forest sheltering wild animals, including elephants and tigers. The limits of Alaungpaya's city extended north only to the Sule, not the Shwedagon. He did, however, make offerings, including four prayer halls on the platform. For the dedication ceremony, princesses, princes, ministers, lords and their retinues accompanied the king.

King Hsinbyushin spent six years repairing damage from the 1768 earthquake. He also raised the height of the *stupa* to 99 metres, replaced the Mon *hti* with a Myanmar *hti*, and covered the pagoda with gold leaf equal to his weight of 170 pounds. The *hti* had 600 silver bells, some of which weighed 17 and a half pounds. Fifteen were made of gold, decorated with jewels. One gold

In the mid-nineteenth century the *pyat-that* were much less ornate than they are today.

147

bell weighed six pounds. All bells were inscribed with the name of the donor. More than 15,000 diamonds and gems were placed on the *hti*, the cone, the vane and the orb. The pagoda repairs used over 10 million bricks, 100,000 brass and 100,000 iron screws, 3,538 gold and over 5,000 silver plates. The *hti* alone measured nearly forty feet, bringing the height of the pagoda to 103 metres.

The son of Hsinbyushin, King Singu, again regilded the pagoda and donated a sixteen-ton bronze bell in 1778. Singu's bell [18] is also known as the bell of 'great sound' or Maha-ganda. Charms and signs are fixed above the bell to prevent any harm coming to it. An inscription in Burmese requests that Singu Min might obtain Nirvana as a result of this act of merit, stating in part:

"Let him not meet with that towards which he has no mental disposition and for which he has no desire. When Arimettiya, the last Buddha, shall be revealed, let him have the revelation that he may become a nat supreme of the three rational existences. Let the nats who guard the royal city, the palace, the umbrella, the nats who all around guard the empire, the provinces, the villages, the nats who guard the monuments of the Divine Hair around the hill Tambagutta, together with the nats governing the earth and space, and all rational beings throughout the universe utter praises and accept the supplications."

Prayer posts are generally topped with the mythical *hintha* birds.

British fortifications, a sad reminder of the colonial appropriation of the Shwedagon.

The Pagoda during the British Occupation

During the first Anglo-Burmese war in 1824, the Shwedagon platform was used as a barracks and artillery station. Monastic libraries were also pillaged. The Burmese troops, under the command of Maha Bandula, advanced towards the pagoda in December. On the north side, they were only separated by a tank that British troops called the Scotch Tank, as the water was thought to be medicinal. The Burmese called it the 'Blood Washing Tank', Thway-say-kan, as they used it to wash the blood from their swords. British troops eventually defeated the Burmese, occupying the pagoda until 1826 when it was turned over to the new Burmese mayor, the Myo Wun.

During the British occupation of the pagoda, Singu's bell was removed. Like de Brito's earlier attempt, the bell sank in the middle of the river. It was recovered in 1826. Some accounts say this was done by tying it with ropes attached to a ship moored over it at low tide; as the tide rose, the bell was lifted. Other versions say that fixing a large number of bamboo poles to the bell, allowing it to float to the surface raised the bell. In any case, the bell now rests on the northwest corner of the pagoda platform.

Following the return of the pagoda to Burmese control, King Tharawaddy in 1841 established a town at Dagon, north of Alaungpaya's town near the river. King Tharawaddy was the younger brother of King Bagyidaw (r. 1819-37), having served with General Maha Bandula during the First Anglo-Burmese War. He acquired the name Shwebo Min, as he was at Shwebo when King Bagyidaw asked him to take the throne. King Tharawaddy came south from Amarapura in 1841 to build a new city at Yangon, north of Alaungpaya's earlier city. Tharawaddy's city was known as Okkalapa, with the a formal name of Aung Myey Yan Hnin ('victory in the land expelling the enemy').

He presented a bell of 40 tons, which is on the northwest corner of the pagoda [33]. In the 1890s the pavilion looked to be much the same as it is today. Tharawaddy bell was not completed until after the king's death, being cast in 1843, making it the last royal bell made for the Shwedagon. It is some 2.5 high. The bell is also known as the Maha-ti-ssada-ganda meaning 'the bell, which produces a great sound'. It bears an inscription in Pali and Burmese, recording the deeds of the king in support of Buddhism. The inscription, the longest on any bell, is written in four panels each surrounded by floral motifs. It tells the story of Buddha in a previous existence, as the hermit Thumedha. The hermit was blessed by the Buddha Dipankara, and was then born as Prince Siddartha. King Tharawaddy inherited this legacy, donating the bell as one of his works of merit. He prays in the inscription to become a Buddha, sharing

Singu's bell and Tharawaddy's bell recall the long tradition of bronze casting In Myanmar, dating back to the country's prehistoric period.

A cascade of roofs and *pyat-that* that lead up to the main shrine.

the merit with relatives, teachers, friends, *nats*, and all other beings.

In 1852, fighting broke out once more with the British. Fifteen warships with 6,000 men arrived in Rangoon on 1 April. The brother of Jane Austen, the British author, commanded the naval force. By mid-April the British controlled the Shwedagon, having successfully moved up the little-fortified east staircase. The Burmese retreated down the south and west entries. British troops were to occupy parts of the Shwedagon for the next 77 years, until 1929.

In 1853, although part of the platform continued to be occupied by British forces, the care of the shrine was returned to Burmese control. Further donations were made by King Mindon in the following years. The *hti* donated by the King in 1871 was brought from Mandalay to Yangon by boat, stopping along the way, as further donations were made to the *hti* and its jeweled vane. A committee was established to oversee the installation, carried out by erecting a scaffolding of bamboo and series of pulleys. Pearn notes that 50,000 bamboos and seventy boatloads of cane were used for the scaffolding. Some 300 workmen were employed in the first month and 500 in the second to complete the raising of the new *hti*. Made of wrought iron, with seven tiers, it weighed over a ton. U Pe Maung Tin, in his Annual Report, noted that some 100,000 people were present on and around the pagoda platform for its installation. Despite British fears of a disturbance, the religious consecration and celebration concluded without problem.

Offerings of gold leaf for gilding were made in 1872 and 1875 – 18,000 and 5,000 packets. In 1873, the king built a monastery at the foot of the hill on the east, although it was necessary to lease the land from the British. Ten years earlier, the Thai king had also leased land to erect a rest house.

The Shwedagon Board of Trustees was formed in 1885. By 1898, the trustees were elected by the Burmese rather than being appointed. In the early years of the 20th century, the pagoda continued to be a focal point in Burmese opposition to British rule. Two organizations, the Young Men's Buddhist Association and the General Council of Burmese Associations annually included resolutions protesting military presence at the Shwedagon. The Young Men's Buddhist Association also passed a resolution in 1917 forbidding footwear on the pagoda, and in 1919 the colonial authorities also ordered that footwear be removed, except for government employees.

In 1920, students, as part of an effort to establish an independent administration from the universities of British India, held commemorative ceremonies at the Shwedagon on an unofficial 'national' day. This custom continued throughout the struggle for independence and remains part of the Union Day celebrations. The Commemorative Column [sw corner] was erected in memory of this university student revolt against British rule. It carries inscriptions in Myanmar, English, French and Russian.

In 1929, British soldiers buried on the platform were transferred to military cemeteries, and in November of that year, responsibility for the pagoda was passed to the Pagoda Trustees. This was celebrated with the re-opening of the western staircase, which had been reserved for military use. However, disputes continued, and for example, in 1939 British colonial police in boots raided strike camps on the pagoda. The Shwedagon was a rallying point for the mass meetings held by Bogyoke Aung San in 1945 and 1946.

Two days before independence was achieved on 4 January 1948, the Pagoda Trustees guided the last British governor around the Shwedagon. In 1970, the Trustees undertook major repairs, conserving the *hti* of King Mindon. More than a thousand bells suspended from the *hti* were removed, and their inscriptions recorded. New bells were donated as well: 1344 gold bells, 158 gold bells set with precious stones, and 3745 silver bells. Jewelry given to the pagoda amounted to 71 kilograms of gold (4380 ticals, 158 lbs), 28 kilos of gold and gems, and 410 kilos of silver. Gilding now takes place regularly, with 28,000 packets of gold leaf applied up to the level of the moldings, above which the pagoda is plated with gold.

The Pagoda since 1948

The Pagoda Trustees are today a nine-member board, some elected by the Buddhist community of Yangon, and some appointed by the government. To be eligible, the candidate must be a Buddhist between 40 and 60 years old, having lived in Yangon for at least three years, possesses property, and not have been convicted of any crime. All Buddhist residents of Yangon, of at least 18 years of age, who are neither monks nor recluses, may vote for the trustees. The list of tasks assigned to the trustees dates back to the duties formulated by Queen Shin Saw Bu in the 15th century. These included officials to care for various parts of the pagoda, from the treasury to the orchestras and the sweepers. The trustees now have the authority to repair all existing buildings, appoint watchmen, manage all offerings to the pagoda, and with the permission of the Chief Commissioner, to put up new buildings.

In 1972, the pagoda had a permanent staff of 88 assisted by 32 voluntary associations. The trustees receive guidance from an Advisory Board of nine abbots. Income to pay the pagoda employees is obtained from a variety of sources, including donation boxes, donations for particular purposes, and

A glimpse of the banana bud through the tiered roofs of *pyat-thats*.

151

Offerings of rice to the *Sangha* during one of the Shwedagon's many festivals.

bonds donated by devotees. In 1971, the assets of the pagoda were 7.3 million *kyat*; in addition land totaling 113.844 acres has been granted to the pagoda.

The office of the Pagoda Trustees [43] is on the south side of the platform. There is also a museum containing images donated to the pagoda [44]. A *tazaung* in front of the Pagoda Trustees Office provides a resting-place for important visitors. Also found here are the Tazaung of the Yaungdawbwin Athin and the Weneyathuka Yegyanzin Athin founded in 1909 and 1905, respectively.

There are many associations who have been allowed to build pavilions on the Shwedagon platform. One of these is the Chinese Merited Association. whose Prayer Pavilion [4] was first built in 1898 by the Chinese Merited Association of Yangon. It houses 28 small images of the Buddha, recalling the 28 previous Buddhas. It sits beside a Chinese-style *tazaung*, containing a marble image carved after that at the Kyauk-taw-gyi pagoda near Mandalay.

The Zeidi Yangana Association [25] is the headquarters of an association that donates rice to the monks of Yangon. The association has a large library of books and manuscripts (6,000 volumes in 1948, 7500 in the 1960s). Previously a pavilion known as Ma Bwa's pavilion was located here, housing King Mindon's *hti* before it was raised. Next to this is the charitable labour association, the Thukhakayi Athin, which sweeps and washes the pagoda platform once a week.

Female sweepers clean and wash the marble platform once a week.

393
SHOAY DAGONE PAGODA RANGOON.

P. Klier
Rangoon

A small group of musicians perform on the pagoda platform.

THE MANY-VALUED SIGNIFICANCE OF SHWEDAGON

U Win Pe

This series of photographs from the mid to late nineteenth century illustrate the many radical changes to the southern entry over the years.

The Shwemawdaw pagoda in Bago.

The Mahamuni image in Mandalay.

Myanmar has often been referred to as the land of pagodas, but among the many thousands, both big and small, none has greater significance than the Shwedagon, the country's premier shrine. Other shrines are also highly revered such as the Shwemawdaw shrine at Bago, some 50 miles to the north-east of the Shwedagon. It is of a similar size and structure, being even a little taller though with a shorter plinth perimeter. Built in the 10th century, it was the main shrine of the capital city of Hanthawaddy, the Mon kingdom which stretched across the Ayeyawaddy Delta, along the banks of the estuaries of the Sittang and Thanlwin Rivers and down the coastal strip to Dawei. However, while revering the Shwemawdaw, the Mon kings gave equal support and adoration to the Shwedagon.

Further down the coast from Bago and a little inland lies the Kyaiktyo, the Pagoda of the Golden Rock (*see page 119*), perched precariously on the edge of a precipice, and visited annually by some hundred thousand pilgrims willing to endure a seven mile trek through the jungle. Then there is the famous Mahamuni, the great image at Mandalay, brought over with difficulty from Rakhine in the 18th century. Legend relates how the Buddha breathed life into this great image. Nevertheless, despite the reverence in which these sites are held none receives greater devotion than the Shwedagon. Four types of pagodas can be distinguished. One enshrines the personal relics of the Buddha such as the Sacred Hairs of the Shwedagon, the Tooth at Kandy in Sri Lanka and in Beijing, and the cremated elements. The second type enshrines the *Dhamma*, or the Buddha's teaching, with quotations inscribed on gold or silver plates such as the popular *Ye Dhamma hetuppabhava*, That:

> *"Whatsoever are produced from a cause,*
> *Of these the Tathagato tells the cause,*
> *And that which is the cessation of these*
> *Thus the Great Recluse declares."*

The third type of pagoda enshrines the utensils and other utilities of the Buddha such as his water dipper or staff, while the fourth type enshrines images of the Buddha creation in dedication to him.

According to the type of Theravadan Buddhism practised in Myanmar, 28 Buddhas have so far attained Enlightment in this world-age. Shwedagon enshrines the staff of Kakussandha (the 25th Buddha), the water-dipper of Konagamana (the 26th Buddha), the bathing garment of Kassapa (the 27th Buddha) and the Sacred Hairs of Gottama (the 28th). Being the only pagoda to enshrine the relics of four successive Buddhas it is easy to understand why the Shwedagon is held in such reverence and why it is often called the 'Shrine of the Four Sacred Relics'. Added significance comes from its location in the capital city of Myanmar. Furthermore, throughout history it has been believed that whoever performed meritorious acts at the Shwedagon would earn great merit. The relationship between the former king of Myanmar and the Shwedagon has also been extremely close as it has long believed that whichever king held Shwedagon would have power over the area. Numerous kings and queens have made lavish donations to the pagoda and even those kings whose palaces were in Upper Myanmar would come occasionally to gild the pagoda and embellish it with bells, *htis* and precious stones.

The glass mosaic inlay is complemented by the carved wooden tracery around the entry, and the elaborate wooden roof.

Images of the Buddha, large and small are gathered together, arranged much as they are today (*see page 19*). One standing image in the background contrasts with the more usual seated form.

Buddhism

Buddhism came to Myanmar from India many hundreds of years ago and has remained central to the life of every Burmese. Most Burmese men will enter the monkhood, the *Sangha*, for a short period, while women may attain merit by making offerings of food and other useful items to the monks. In addition, it is believed that much merit will accrue from the construction or renovation of temples and pagodas. On an individual level the practice of meditation is very widespread among the Burmese people. Thus among those visiting the Shwedagon while some are making offerings and some are meditating, almost all are Buddhists paying their respects to the relics and recalling the Buddha's teaching. With this in mind, the many-valued significance of the Shwedagon to the people of Myanmar cannot be appreciated without some basic understanding of Buddhism.

The Life of the Buddha

The 28th Buddha of our era, commonly referred to simply as 'The Buddha' was born Prince Gotama Siddartha in a kingdom on the border of Nepal and India in 543 BC. His father, the king, wanted his son to be happy and surrounded the prince with all kinds of youthful pleasures and beautiful things, at the same time keeping him sequestered from anything which could disturb or upset him. However, the kings efforts were in vain as one day the prince came upon an old man with shrivelled skin, a bent back, toothless jaws and dim eyes. The Prince was shocked to learn that he too would one day become like that old man if he lived long enough. Then he came upon a sick man, groaning in agony and unable to rise up from where he lay. Thus the Prince realised that all flesh was subject to sickness and fevers. Finally the Prince saw a corpse being carried to the cremation ground, followed by grieving mourners and he learned that this was the end which came to all living things. Thus Prince Gotama realised that the world is full of suffering and anguish, that youth ends in old age, pleasure in pain and life in death. Nevertheless, feeling that there must be a way to end such suffering and to help humankind out of this sorrowful condition, he determined to set out to search for the way. Thus at the age of 29 he left the palace and his wife and new-born child in order to renounce the world.

For six years he practised the severest austerities, until he realised that he would not achieve the truth he sought by such extreme measures, which he later likened to trying to make a knot in the air. Taking food once more he went to meditate under the Bodhi-tree. Then the Blessed One during the first watch of the night meditated on the process of conditioned genesis both forward and reversed. In this He saw the origin of the whole aggregation of sorrow and also the way to the cessation of this sorrow. Having understood this matter the Blessed One breathed forth this cry:

> *"When separate-natures truly are manifested to the strenuous*
> *contemplative holy man*
> *Then all his doubt vanish, because he understands nature that has*
> *a cause."*

Then the Blessed One during the middle watch of the night meditated further on the process of conditioned genesis and breathed forth this cry:

> *"When separate-natures truly are manifested to the strenuous*
> *contemplative holy man*
> *Then all his doubts vanish, because he has known the destruction of*
> *the bases."*

Then the Blessed One during the third watch of the night meditated further

A variety of *htis* – round, square, fringed, adorn this image of the Buddha.

on the process of conditioned genesis and breathed forth this cry:

> *"When separate-natures truly are manifested to the strenuous contemplative holy man*
> *He stands and scatters the army of Mara the Tempter even as the sun lighting the heavens."*

The Blessed One perceived and understood that His mind was liberated from the taint of lust, the taint of individual existence, the taint of wrong view, and the taint of ignorance. He knew existence was ended, the holy life was being lived and that what must be done had been done. The Buddha then went to the Deer Park at Benares and discoursed on the Four Noble Truths and the Eightfold Middle Path to attaining enlightenment and the cessation of suffering.

The Four Noble Truths

Existence is sorrowful, decay is sorrowful, disease is sorrowful, death is sorrowful, union with the unpleasing is sorrowful, separation from the pleasing is sorrowful, the wish which one does not fulfil is sorrowful; in brief, the five aggregates of body, sensation, concept, will and conciousness is sorrowful.
This is the First Noble Truth of Sorrow (*Dukkha*).
Recurring craving associated with enjoyment and desire, seeking enjoyment again and again; namely, the craving for sense pleasure, the craving for individual existence, the craving for super-existence.
This is the Second Noble Truth of the Origin of Sorrow.
The cessation of this craving so that no remnant or trace of it remains, its abandonment, its renunciation, liberation and detachment.
This is the Third Noble Truth of the Cessation of Sorrow.
The Fourth Noble Truth is the Middle Way, or the Eightfold Path leading to the cessation of sorrow.

The Eightfold Path

Right View is knowledge of the Four Noble Truths.
Right Thinking is the will to practise renunciation of illusion.
Right Speech is abstinence from false speaking, malicious speech, harsh speech, frivolous talk.
Right Action is abstinence from taking life, from what is not given, from sexual misconduct.
Right Living is living by right discipline.
Right Effort is making efforts so that unrighteous qualities not having arisen may not arise, or having arisen may be abandoned; and righteous qualities not

having arisen may arise, or having arisen may have full development.
Right Mindfulness is mindfulness of body, sensation, mind and *Dhamma*
elements.
Right Concentration is gaining and dwelling in the *jhanas* and *samadhi*.

Devotion

The Buddha did not attain Englightenment through striving in just one life
but over a hundred thousand world ages during which he completed the
Ten Perfections – the Perfection of Giving; the Perfection of Morality; the
Perfection of Renunciation; the Perfection of Wisdom; the Perfection of Effort;
the Perfection of Patience; the Perfection of Truthfulness; the Perfection of
Resolution; the Perfection of Loving Kindness; the Perfection of Equanimity.

The Jatakas
During these lives which are told in the Jataka Tales of which there are 550.
He is referred to as a Bodhisattva (a being who delays becoming a Buddha in
order to help humankind). Examples of certain of the Jataka Tales showing the
Blessed Nature of the Buddha before enlightenment are given below.
Certain incidents are more popular than others and several are illustrated at
the Shwedagon.

When the Bodhisattva was King Thiwi, he gave away hundreds of
thousands of pounds of silver, but finding this still insufficient, he even gave
away both his eyes. Then as King Wethandaya, he gave away not only his
kingdom but his wife and children. Sometimes the Buddha was an animal.
Thus as Thinkhapala, the dragon-serpent, he sat observing the precepts on a
mound. Passersby poked him with lances, while others drove wedges into his
nose and attaching ropes carried him away on their shoulders. But even
though as a dragon Thinkhapala could have scorched them all with one fiery
puff from his nostrils, he faithfully observed the precepts until he died.
As Mahazanaka, the Bodhisattva was an exemplar both of the practice of
renunciation and the requirement of effort, while as Mahawthada he practised
the perfection of wisdom.

Another somewhat chilling *jataka*, illustrates the perfection of patience
and relates how the Bodhisattva even as a young baby could bear tremendous
pain. One day the father of the baby Prince Dhammapala visited his son while
his mother, his queen was bathing him. Absorbed in her task, she did not
notice the king. Fearing that if she disregarded her husband now when the

The woodcarving tradition of Myanmar is long-standing and
unique, epitomised in the grace and beauty of the *pyat-that*.

Page 162
Change has been a constant part of the Shwedagon's
architecture – not only modifications to the main *stupa* but the
many other aspects of the platform such as the Golden
Umbrellas and the Holy Well.

163

baby was still young, she might show even greater lack of interest once her son was older, he called for the baby and cut off his arms and legs. The child did not cry out in either pain or anger. The queen cried out "Now the child is limbless, he cannot be a danger to you. May I take him away?" A response that elicited such anger from the king that he chopped off the baby's head, causing the queen to die immediately of a broken heart.

The perfection of resolution is illustrated by the tale of the Bodhisattva Prince Temi, who desirous of renouncing the world and not becoming a king, pretended to be deaf and dumb. Though various means were devised to test his faculties, he did not swerve from his resolve and thereby attained the perfection he sought.

The Tripitaka – The Three Essentials of Buddhism

The Buddha
The Buddha is possessed of nine Attributes. The Buddha is worthy of special
veneration. The Buddha truly comprehends all the *dhammas* through his own
intellect and insight and is thus full enlightened. The Buddha possesses
supreme knowledge and practises perfect morality. The Buddha speaks only
what is beneficial and true. The Buddha knows all the three worlds of humans,
devas and Brahmas. The Buddha is incomparable in taming those who deserve
to be tamed. The Buddha is the incomparable Teacher of *devas* and humans.
The Buddha is the enlighted One who knows and teaches the Four Noble
Truths. The Buddha is the Most Exalted One.

The Dhamma
The *Dhamma* taught by the Buddha possesses Six Attributes. The *Dhamma* is
well expounded, being good in the beginning, the middle and the end. The
Dhamma is personally appreciable here and now. The *Dhamma* is not delayed
in its results, its fruits are given immediately. The *Dhamma* invites
investigation, saying, "This is the way that it is comprehended and realized,
you may practise thus, comprehend and realize. The *Dhamma* is realized and
experienced by the Ariya (Noble Ones) individually by their own efforts and
practice.

The Sangha
The disciples of the Buddha, the *Sangha* (monks) are endowed with right
practice; they are endowed with straightforward uprightness; they are endowed
with right effort with Nirvana in mind. They are endowed with unfailing
correctness in practice. The *Sangha*, consisting of eight categories or four
pairs of Ariya, are worthy of receiving offerings brought from afar; they are
worth of receiving offerings specially set aside for guests; they are worthy of
offerings donated for well being in the next existence; they are worthy of
receiving obeisance; they are an incomparable fertile field for all to sow the
seed of merit.

Appreciative of and inspired by Buddha's efforts in the Ten Perfections and the
desire to infuse one's mind with veneration to the holy attributes of the
Buddha, the *Dhamma* and the *Sangha*, people go to worship at the
Shwedagon. One earns more merit by donating to a monk of righteous
conduct than by giving to a drunkard because one can better attune one's

Not only did styles of wood carving evolve, new pavilions and
shrines have been added to the platform over the years.

So much space displaced
great goldbell of sky
holding the sun in a dome of brightness
through all the unperceived spheres of reality

So much weight and height
and amplitude
dilation of dome gathered inwards
to well above the annulations in a bulb
then rise along the fretwork pinnacle
to jewelled point

Encompassing in its capriciousness
not the satiety of oneself
but the fullness of other non-self.

U Win Pe

mind to purity and morality in the first case. In like manner one can better attune one's mind to veneration and reverence when praying at such a holy pagoda such as Shwedagon. Thus visitors can surrender themselves to the powerful presence of the pagoda, pay hommage with reverence and diminished pride once, twice and thrice to the Buddha, the *Dhamma* and the *Sangha* so that the faults and misconducts of body speech and thought be eliminated and not repeated. May their prayer result in avoidance of birth in the four nether worlds, escape from the three scourges, in avoidance of dwelling in the eight unworthy locations or being harassed by the five enemies, the four impairments, and the five losses. May this act contribute to the attainment of Knowledge of the Way, Fruition and Nirvana.

Many of the *tazaung* are now larger, but no less elaborate than in former times.

Giving

History records a continuous stream of kings, both Mon and Burmese, from Lower and Upper Burma who came to rebuild the pagoda after earthquakes, to renovate, to raise still higher, to offer gold equivalent of their body weight or that of their queen, to gild the pagoda, to install *htis*, to contribute jewels and precious stones, to build devotional halls, or to assign personnel to maintain and manage the pagoda.

Names which stand out are Queen Shin Saw Bu, the only regnant queen of Myanmar, whose devotion raised the pagoda to nearly its present height and who requested to look upon it in her dying moments. Then there are kings Dhammaceti, Singu Min and Tharawaddy who donated huge bells, or Hsinbyushin and Mindon, the next to last king of Myanmar, who erected *htis*. The first time the *hti* was hoisted under the auspices of the common people was in 1610. The present *hti*, though created in Mandalay with a large contribution from King Mindon was hoisted not by his commission which transported the *hti* from Mandalay to Yangon but by the common people of Yangon, Bama, Kayin, Mon and Shan. It now stands at the top of the *stupa* to grace the structure with beauty and elegance.

The people also donated bells, not as huge as those of Dhammaceti, Singumin or King Tharawaddy but big enough. They are in various places on the platform, 27 in all. Seven of these were offered by monks, one monk being from Bangkok. 17 were offered by common people, traders, rice mill owners, land owners and their families. One bell was offered by a group of 30 people, who shared the merit earned with parents, grandparents, relatives, friends, all kinds of guardian spirits of earth, water and air, comfortable beings and suffering beings. They also inscribed the bell with the wish that the merit would stand them in good stead and contribute towards the attainment of Nirvana. Smaller bells were also offered and were hung on the frames of the *hti* and which tinkle in the wind with the soft spoken sound of peace. Hundreds of such bells have been donated but not all can be hung because of the weight. The donors come from all parts of the country and belong to various trades. The dates of hanging are clustered round those years when a scaffold is contructed to the top of the stupa for repairs to earthquake damage or the installation of a new *hti*. Some of the bells are gem-studded but most gems and precious stones are either attached to the vane or are enshrined.

There is much joy in giving and people are anxious that they might miss and opportunity to give. Duncan gives an account of the reception in Yangon to King Mindon's *hti*:

The base of this sacred pole is adorned with various mythological figures.

Some parts, such as Singu's bell and the honouring of the pagoda by annual re-gilding, are long-standing traditions.

The Elder Brother Pagoda is situated in the northeast corner of the platform.
At right, elaborate *dagung-daing* are topped with bejewelled elephants or
miniature *pyat-thats*.

"There were numerous depots where were freely given sherbet, cakes, green tea, cheroots and various condiments.

"The personal sacrifice of the people can be seen by the amount already mentioned as having been contributed in Rangoon, but the sincerity and good faith with which their offerings were made could be judged only by witnessing the anxiety with which they crowded to the place set apart for their reception.

"An old woman totters up with a small piece of gold which would be taken with as much care and form as the most valuable gift; a girl nervously pulls off a pair of handsome earrings, whose value will entitle them to an immediate place on the vane; a man takes off his ruby ring and adds it to the heap. And so the spirit of sacrifice works."

The giving was not confined to bells and jewelleries. Cardinal devotional halls, prayer halls, cave shrines and small pagodas were erected. Some were donated by individual families such as the elegant Dr. U Nyo's Hall, the finely decorated Chan Mah Phwe's Hall or the Sawlapaw Pagoda. The western stairway was built with funds collected from sellers at the Theingyizay Market at the rate of two pice (1/2 a rupee) per day, while the beautiful hall to the east of the Mahabodhi Temple was built by the daily contribution of two *pice* from the shopkeepers of the Strand Market.

There are five qualities of virtuous giving:

1. Giving with belief in karma and its productivity in results.
2. Giving with respect and reverence
3. Giving performed at an appropriate time such as offering special robes to monks during the Kathin ceremony once a year. Not offering food to monks after noon time.
4. Giving without clinging or attachment to what one gives.
5. Giving in a manner not to hurt another person.

One gives in the belief that it will contribute toward the final liberation of Nirvana. One also understands that its fruits can be enjoyed in existences before that final liberation. Above all, giving is useful because it causes attrition of the attachment to self. When one gives, one is selfless; one is freed from identification with the notion of self which, in any case an illusion, is the result of ignorance.

The scale of the main *stupa* in comparison with the surrounding shrines is very apparent.

Precepts

Myanmar people generally make their vow of five absinences in front of the household shrines found in every home:

1. Abstention from killing
2. Abstention from taking what is not given.
3. Abstention from sexual misconduct.
4. Abstention from falsehood.
5. Abstention from the taking of intoxicants.

On special days like Full Moon Day or a birthday, they like to take the vows before a sacred image or pagoda. On such a day they may take the eight precepts:

1. Abstention from killing
2. Abstention from taking what is not given.
3. Abstention from sex.
4. Abstention from falsehood.
5. Abstention from intoxicants.
6. Abstention from food after midday.
7. Abstention from dancing, singing, playing musical instruments, watching shows, wearing flowers or perfumes.
8. Abstention from using high and luxurious beds or seats.

Nowadays a ninth vow is taken which does not involve an abstention but is a positive undertaking to develop a loving mind towards all sentient beings. Some people also vow to abstain from food which involves the taking of life, an abstention commonly understood as being vegetarian. In the West some vegetarians eat eggs, but in Myanmar a vegetarian will not eat eggs or food made therefrom because of the embryo in the egg. People may vow to be vegetarian for a month, a year or for life. Some choose to be vegetarian just on the weekday of their birth. People come to the Shwedagon to reaffirm their vow of avoiding food which involves the taking of life.

Meditation

Many people come to meditate under the powerful influence of the Shwedagon, a power which has been generated by hundreds of thousands of devotees meditating through the centuries. Some people tell rosaries, some recite the suttas, some repeat mantras. Some come to meditate on loving-kindness, spreading love till it covers all beings. Some come to meditate on the Nine Attributes of Buddha, some to be mindful of in-breathing and out-breathing (*anapana*) and some to be mindful of the sensations in the body, the aches, shooting sharpness, the pain. Meditation is of two kinds: contemplation, which is of conceptual objects, notions or ideas and leads to *Samatha*. Mindfulness of in-breathing and out-breathing or sensations leads to *Vipassana* insight.

There are special spots on the pagoda where people believe the influence of the pagoda is most powerful. One is on the upper terrace in front of the Ruby-Eyed Buddha. Another spot is Queen Shin Saw Bu's shrine situated in the north-west section at the shrine of the Sun and Moon. Frequently, meditators will have their own favourite spots which could be in the cardinal *tazaung* or in one of the many prayer halls.

Elaborate wood-carving and stuccowork create a rich background for meditation and prayer.

A joyful *deva* stands before deeply and elaborately carved wooden columns of a pavilion.

Solace or Boon

Many people come to the Shwedagon for solace. As Buddha revealed in the First Noble Truth in the First Sermon of the Turning of the Wheel of Law, the rising of the five aggregates of body, sensation, conception, volition and conciousness cause sorrow. Thus, humans being composed of the five aggregates are bound to suffer sorrow. One way to alleviate that sorrow is to go to the pagoda and find solace in prayer and giving, by offering candles, incense, flowers, water, a paper umbrella, a paper pennant, or gold leaf.

Some people consult an astrologer who advises which objects should be offered at which planetary post at what time on which day of the week. The more popular planetary posts are the Saturday post in the south-west corner of the *stupa* plinth and the late Wednesday post in the north-west corner. Indeed, the Saturday post is so popular that it is sometimes difficult to find room to make an offering and say a prayer.

Rituals are in some cases performed in order to receive a boon or to fulfil a wish, even though the Buddha in fact taught that:

"Oneself is the refuge; what other refuge would there be?"

"By oneself along is evil done, by oneself is one defiled. By oneself is evil left undone, by oneself alone is one purified. Purity and impurity depends on oneself. Noone can purify another."

Thus the Buddha emphasized self-reliance, but human nature being weak, seeks help in externals, in others than oneself.

Loki and *Lokuttara*

On the Shwedagon platform may be found both Buddhist practices, *lokuttara*, and non-Buddhist practices, known as *loki* practices. As already discussed, Buddhist practices, or *lokuttara*, pertains to the removal of ignorance of the three characteristics of impermanance, *dukkha* and *anatta* (non-self), the practice of *vipassana* insight for the attainment of *Magga* (the Way), *Phala* (Fruition) and *Nirvana* (Extinction of the Flame of Rebirth). It is also concerned with devotion to the Buddha as teacher, with the Ten Perfections and Nine Attributes, to the *Dhamma* as Guide with the Six Attributes and the *Sangha* with the Nine Attributes as exemplar and fertile field for the sowing of merit.

Loki, on the other hand, is concerned with advantages in this worldly life, the propitiation of spirits for protection or boon, the practice of ritual as for supernatural powers in the next existence in which one may exercise those powers. *Weizas* and *nats* are *loki*. For people interested in *loki* practices and the occult, there are various shrines such as Shin Issagona, the wizard, and shrines for Bo Bo Gyi and the Shwedagon guardian *nat*, and the *tazaungs* for Bo Bo Aung and Bo Min Gaung.

Devas and *chinthe* (the mythical lion) guard the entry to some of the many small stupas on the platform.

Dagon Relic Shrine on Singutt Hill
When two brothers with deep adoration
Offered honey cakes after Day Six
The Enlightened One allowed the Sacred Hairs
Be adored on this Hilltop. So they were enshrined,
A stupa dedicated to the Enlightened One.
May my prayer be realized.

Nawadei, 16th century

The richness of the Shwedagon's architecture befits the sacredness of the shrine. Images, *stupas*, *pyat-that* and *tazaung* all combine to create the unique atmosphere of the pagoda platform.

Art and Craft

Shwedagon and its founding legend have inspired drama, song, painting and poetry. The pagoda itself has so much beauty, magnificence and serenity. The beauty of its unique form has been copied in several pagodas erected in the outlying states, enabling those who cannot visit Yangon to experience for themselves the beauty and serenity of the Shrine of the Relics of Four Buddhas.

The traditional nature of the architecture of this ancient pagoda is reflected in the newly renovated stairways done in an authentic renaissance of traditional Myanmar craft. They constitute a proper complement to the golden magnificence fo the pagoda.

The pagoda is surrounded by the cardinal devotional halls, the stairway entrance halls and the prayer halls or *tazaungs*, bell halls and cave shrines. The *tazaungs* are of two types: *yun tazaung* which has multi-tiered roofs but no spire and *pyat-that tazaung* which has multi-tiered roofs which become smaller as they rise and end in a spire. Devotional halls and the prayer halls have wood carvings on the ridges and eaves, some of which are specially graceful as in Chan Mah Pee's Hall and Rakhine Tazaung. There are screen carvings on the spandrels luxuriant with floral scrollwork. One beautiful specimen is the spandrel on the northern Devotional Hall. Most screen carvings have scenes from the Jataka Tales, legends or stories worked into the foliage. The screen carving in the Carousel Hall gives an effect of lacquerwork. Another technique is to combine woodcarvings and paintings to produce panels with a three-dimensional effect. Yet another important decorative element is the glass mosaic on columns and ceilings creating an impression of luxury and magnificence.

Numerous figures ornament the platform. The *chinthe* or lion is a familiar figure, while the *manuthiha* or 'man-lion' has special significance. Elsewhere a *bilu* or ogre acts as a guardian figure. *Nats* are everywhere, with Sakka being the most common. Then there is Vathondari *nat* rinsing water from her hair and bearing witness to the charities exemplified in the Bodhisattva's many lives. Bell hooks are often decorated with *nagas* or serpents. On the southern Devotional Hall the *pyinsa-rupa* is formed from the parts of five animals, birds and fish. Finally there are the multitudes of Buddha images, often shaded with exquisitely decorated umbrellas. Some of these images are expressionless while some reflect the wisdom and peace when the fires of the defilements are extinguished.

Millions of images of the Shwedagon are found throughout Myanmar in homes, offices and monasteries confirming its central role as a mythic image of power, protection and national unity.

Power and Nationalism

Though not intended, over the centuries Shwedagon has become a symbol of power. Whoever held the Shwedagon could claim sovereignty over the surrounding Ayeyawaddy Delta and the Sittang River basin. But at first it was the Relics which attracted kings. Thus the Pyu king Duttabaung came to seize them but the power of the pagoda was such that the king simply embellished the pagoda and returned home. Such an incident was repeated with King Anawratha of Bagan (Pagan) in the eleventh century, when the king donated gold and silver umbrellas and returned to Bagan. In later centuries, the centre of power was at Bago, but whoever conquered Bago always embellished the Shwedagon.

The British were the ones who turned the Shwedagon Hill into a citadel during the First Burmese War of 1826. In 1852, they occupied the Hill and buried their dead there, as well as siting a magazine which blew up. The western side of the pagoda was locked and pilgrims were not permitted.

When King Mindon wanted to elevate a new *hti* at the request of the people of Yangon, the British were hesitant, afraid that Mindon's visit to Yangon to hoist the hti would be construed as him exercising sovereignty over Lower Myanmar, already annexed by the British. Finally, they relented with the proviso that the *hti* must be elevated by the people of Yangon. The arrangement was agreed and the people of Yangon earned the admiration of the British officers for their generosity, cooperation, discipline and order.

By 1919, the people could no longer stand the British riding rough-shod over their culture. There were two issues connected with the pagoda. One was the military occupation of a part of the pagoda. The General Council of Burmese Associations and the Young Men's Buddhist Association demanded a clear statement of when the military would vacate the premises. The agitation for this continued until 1929 when the bodies of British soldiers buried on the pagoda were removed and the western stairway transferred into the hands of the Pagoda Trustees. The stairway held in military control for 77 years could now be used by pilgrims. The other issue was that of footwear which had been prohibited since the days of the Myanmar kings. However, after the annexation of Lower Myanmar, the tradition was openly flouted by Europeans and the 'shoe question' became a national issue with nation-wide agitation.

In 1920, students of Myanmar's only university went on strike. The leaders held their planning meeting at the south-west corner of the pagoda, now marked by a stone pillar. Student strikes in 1936 and oil-field workers in 1938 also established strike camps in the rest-houses on Pagoda Hill.

The national anthem was premiered on the hill. In the year 1945 and 1946, at the height of the political struggle which earned the country's freedom, Bogyoke Aung San used the middle terrace of the Pagoda Hill as the venue for mass meetings. In 1946, in response to the call from Bogyoke Aung San virtually all workers came out on strike and yet again camps were established on Pagoda Hill. In one of his speeches Bogyoke Aung San said:

"We have convened at a venue, which, throughout our history has been the quintessence of everything noble and fine and auspicious. So I make a solemn wish for our conference to reflect the nobility and sanctity of the location.
The Singuttara Hill is also where the Four-Relic Sacred Shwedagon rests on its crest. The Shwedagon Zedi testified to the nature of our generosity and the noblest of our desires and its golden glimmer is the light of our yearning for the Supreme goal, Nirvana, where reigns peace and tranquility. If once again we should look at what surrounds us, we will realize that this was where the great movements that fashioned our destiny were born not many years ago. Thus, for us, the peoples of this land, this place is one to be greatly revered."

Shwedagon gives to the people of Myanmar a sense of a nation.
Freedom was won in 1948.

A decorated pulley carries material to the *stupa* during the
most recent restoration in November 1998.

SHWEDAGON – A PERSONAL EXPERIENCE

Nay Htun

I left Yangon in 1956 to study abroad. On the way to Mingladon Airport, I stopped at the Shwedagon to pay my respects and vowed that I would visit it again immediately on my return to the country. I did not realise then that it would be 39 years before I could do so.

My pledge was fulfilled in 1995. One morning at the crack of dawn when it was still not quite light, I went to the very same spot where I had been those many years before. For a weekday, the place was filling up fast with people, young and old, men and women, clearly from all walks of life. As I sat down and began to reflect and contemplate, time and space quickly merged. It seemed as though I had never left the Shwedagon. Was it an illusion or was it reality? Four decades of time telescoped into that instant. All the places I had known were fused into one. This profound feeling of timelessness and spacelessness was heightened by the fact that the sensations I had experienced on the last occasion quickly returned and changed, evoking the same awareness. The Buddha images, the *stupas*, the soft, gentle recitation of the *sutras,* the chanting of mantras, the sight of the people wearing the same style of *aingyi, pasoe,* and *htamein,* the same fragrant smells of freshly cut flowers, the temple bells tinkling in the cool breeze, all combined to recapture the tranquillity, peacefulness, sanctity and nobleness of the Shwedagon. Here, it seemed and felt that avarice, hatred, animosity and ill will, if they had ever existed, evaporated and were replaced by forgiveness, compassion and loving-kindness – *metta.*

Much had changed in the temporal and physical world but at the Shwedagon there was continuity in following the teachings and practices of Buddha; values had been retained alongside cultures and traditions that have existed for generations. The people were paying reverence to the teachings of Buddha and drawing inspiration and strength from his enlightenment. They were seeking a better understanding of the doctrine of truth and reality – the *Dhamma* – and following the code of disciplines – the *vinnaya* – with no ostentatious display of materialism, all in the attempt to break the cycle of *samsara*, of death and rebirth, of the existence of human suffering.

I realised more than ever that Myanmar, known also as the 'Golden Land', is a country with unchanging, golden qualities. It is endowed with priceless resources. And at the Shwedagon, I also realised that its most important resource is its people. This is the strength of the country. This is what helps the country to meet challenges and overcome adversities, as history has shown.

Scaffolding clads the *stupa* during recent restoration in November 1998.

The *hti*, the vane and the diamond orb.

Workers can clamber within the intricate bamboo scaffolding to
regild and repair the various upper parts of the *stupa*.

Glossary

ah-pweh   Wish-granting places.

Ananda   The Buddha's brother who also became one of his disciples.

arahat   Disciple of the Buddha.

anatta   Doctrine of 'no soul'.

Ari Mettaya   The future Buddha.

athin   Association.

bilus   Ogres, often positioned as a guardian figure.

bo bo   Territorial and ancestral spirits.

Bo Bo Aung   An occult master who appears in several shrines at the Shwedagon and is much revered for his ability to read magic diagrams.

Bo Bo Gyi   Territorial guardian spirit of the Shwedagon.

Bodhgaya   The stupa built in Benares on the site of the Buddha's enlightenment.

Bodhi tree   *Ficus religiosa*, the tree under which the Buddha achieved Enlightenment.

Bodhisattva   A being who delays attaining Enlightenment in order to help humankind.

Bo Min Kaung   A *weiza* much revered for his meditational powers who generally appears in small statuettes in various shrines around the pagoda.

Brahma   One of the trinity of Hindu gods.

chinte   Lions.

dagun-daing   Prayer posts; often topped with the *hintha* bird.

Dhamma   The teachings of the Buddha.

devas   Divinities.

dukkha   Suffering arising from the cycle of birth and rebirth endured by living beings.

Erawan   Elephant often shown with three heads who is the mount of the god Indra.

garuda   Half-bird half-man.

galon   See *garuda*; associated with the Sunday born.

Hanthawaddy   The historical name for the Mon capital at Pegu now known as Bago.

hintha   Mythical bird linked in legend with one of the *jatakas*.

hsin   Elephant.

hti   Umbrella used to adorn stupas and the platform; often donated by kings and queens.

Indra   King of the gods.

jatakas   'Birth stories' of which there are 547 recounting the Buddha's previous incarnations.

Kakusandha   First Buddha of our era.

kalasa   An offering vase.

kappa   Buddhist era.

Kassapa   Third Buddha of this era.

khonan angles   Corners with seven angles or folds of equal dimensions, the name meaning pigeon house of a palace.

kinnaya   Mythic creatures which are half-human, half-bird.

Konagamana   Second Buddha of this era.

kwet   Rat, associated with the Thursday born.

kya   Tiger, associated with the Monday born.

Kyaiktyo   A pagoda often linked with Shwedagon built in memory of a hermit prince of that name.

kyaung   Monastery.

Mahayana Buddhism   Sometimes referred to as the Greater Vehicle in which the historical Buddha is one of many Bodhisattvas and Buddhas who have gained enlightenment. Prevalent in Tibet, China and Japan, although Buddhism in Myanmar contains many Mahayanist elements.

Mai Lamu   The legendary mother of King Okkalapa ruler of Dagon, she was born from a fruit.

Mya Shin Shrine   Shrine of the Ruby-eyed Buddha whose image some believe represents the future Buddha.

manuthiha   Human-faced double-bodied lion guardians.

naga   Mythical serpents who inhabit the oceans and guard its riches.

nats   Spirits often associated with particular places. 37 were codified in the 11 century, but many others also exist.

Nirvana   The extinction of suffering through an end to the cycle of rebirth following Enlightenment.

pan trees   Flowering trees in gold and silver presented as offerings to the Buddha.

Pegu Mae Daw   Female nat and royal mother of Pegu.

pice   Small copper coins.

pu   Guinea pig, associated with the Friday born.

pyat-that   tiered roof.

pyinsa-rupa   Mystical animal composed of five different beasts – the tusks and trunk of an elephant, the antlers and legs of a deer, the body of a serpent, a lion's mane and the wings of the *hintha*.

Rahu   Deity who is believed to cause eclipses by swallowing the sun or moon.

Sakka   Lord of the Nats; also known as Thagyarmin. He has evolved from the Hindu god Indra.

Sangha   The Buddhist monkhood.

Sarasvati Hindu goddess and consort of Brahma.

shin Wise monk.

Shin Ajagona Also known as Shin Izzagona, he was an alchemist during the Pagan era.

Shin Ariputta One of the Buddha's disciples.

Shin-byu ceremony Ceremony for young men or boys prior to entering the monkhood.

Shin Moggalana One of the Buddha's disciples.

Shin Thiwali One of the Buddha's disciples who became very popular for his generous and loving nature. Statues of him standing as a monk may be seen at the Shwedagon.

Shin Upako A wise monk living after the time of the Buddha with great meditative powers enabling him to float on the sea. Offerings are made to him in the hope of success in all undertakings and of overcoming obstacles.

Shwe Nan Kyin A female serpent, mother of a daughter with occult powers, who according to certain legends married the king of Thaton.

Tabuang Festival Held in February or March to celebrate the deposit of the hair relics.

tazaung Shrine or devotional hall.

thabaeik Begging or alms bowl.

Tha din Gyut Festival Held in October, this is the Festival of Lights marking the end of the rains.

Thagyarmin, see Sakka.

Theravada Buddhism Sometimes known as the 'Lesser Vehicle' this is the type of Buddhism adopted in Sri Lanka, Myanmar and Thailand, although elements of Mahayana Buddhism are also found in Myanmar.

Thin-gyan Festival The Water Festival which marks the beginning of the New Year in the traditional Myanmar calendar.

Thurathati Female nat, after Sarasvati, consort of Brahma.

Tripitaka The three baskets of Buddhism comprising the Buddha, the *Dhamma* and the *Sangha*.

vipassana Insight meditation.

weiza Occult master.

yadaya An act or donation to fulfill a donation formulated by an astrologer.

zawgyi Alchemist.

zayat Rest house.

CHRONOLOGY

1372 King Byinnya U raises height of pagoda to 60 feet.

1436-51 Kings Byinnyayan (1426-46), Byinnyawaru (1446-50) and Byinnyakyan (1450-53 rebuild pagoda after earthquake. The height of the pagoda is raised to 302 feet, roughly its present height, the extra 24 feet including the superstructure of the *hti*. Queen Shin Saw Bu particularly active in this work.

1451 Queen Shin Saw Bu was the first to gild the pagoda using her own weight in gold (40kg).

1476 Queen Shin Saw Bu and King Dhammaceti embellish Pagoda Hill

1485 Three inscriptions on eastern slope of Singuttara Hill, 50 feet below the platform, were engraved by order of King Dhammaceti. He also measures his weight and his queen's weight in gold and with four times their weight overlays the pagoda with scrollwork and tracery. Casts a great bell.

1492-1526 Reign of King Byinnyayam who further embellishes the umbrella and crown. On 48th birthday installed 48 little pagodas on the base.

1564 Earthquake during eclipse of the sun. Middle stage has to be pulled down and rebuilt.

1583 Account of the pagoda by Gasparo Balbi and Ralph Fitch.

1610 People of Dagon under leadership of Abbot Angebue gild the pagoda.

1613 King Anaukpetlun casts a bronze bell to replace that of King Dhammaceti which the Portuges Felipe de Brito y Nicote had attempted to steal, sinking it in the river in the process.

1619 King Anaukpetlun installs a crown and a *hti* on the pagoda.

1620, 1628, 1644, 1649, 1652 Earthquakes damage *hti*.

1664 Earthquake caused greater damage. Damage to the fabric repaired the following year, and a year after that a new *hti* was hoisted with great ceremony.

1755 King Alaungpaya, the founder of Rangoon, erects four prayer halls on the platform of the pagoda.

1759   King Alaungpaya visits pagoda again, gilding it from the *hti* to the base and constructing a covered stepway.

1768   Earthquake seriously damages the pagoda. The total reconstruction of upper portion took over six years.

1769-1775   King Hsinbyushin oversees the rebuilding. The present mouldings, lotus petals and banana bud section are the work of craftsmen who undertook this restoration. Materials included 3,538 gold plates, over 5,000 silver plates, over 10 million bricks, 100,000 brass screws and 100,000 iron screws. The gilding from top to base took 77 kg of gold equivalent to the king's body weight.

A new *hti* of iron and brass plating was constructed. The *hti*, the cone, the jewelled vane and diamond orb were plated with 44 kg of gold melted down from golden treasures belonging to the king, queen mother and royal princesses. They were then set with 15,038 diamonds and gems. The 356 gold and silver bells recovered when the former top broke off were augmented by a further 32.9 kg of gold and silver bells and these were hung from the *hti*.

Over 600 gold Buddha images and over 7,700 silver images which were recovered when pagoda broke open were re-enshrined.

King Singu Min completed great bell begun by King Hsinbyushin.

1824   First Anglo-Burmese war. British force occupies and fortifies Pagoda Hill. T. A. Trant who accompanied the expedition left excellent description of the Shwe Dagon.

1826   British return Pagoda Hill to Burmese who undertake major repairs.

1841   King Tharawaddy comes to Rangoon intending to build a new town in place of Alaungpaya's town which had been destroyed by fire or decayed. Shwedagon formed north-east corner of town. He regilded the pagoda and cast a new bell.

1852   Second Anglo-Burmese war. Fighting on the pagoda. British force again occupies and fortifies Pagoda Hill. Military and naval officers attempted to loot pagoda much to annoyance of Governor General in Calcutta.

1869   Old Hsinbyushin *hti* now 100 years old and new one requested of King Mindon according to tradition. Old *hti* brought down and gold and ornaments sent to Mandalay for inclusion in new *hti*.

1871   King Mindon's *hti*, vane and diamond orb is installed on the pagoda. Over 214 kg of gold used in its fabrication. British appreciated the significance of the Shwedagon embellishment and feared it represented a claim by the Burmese kings to sovereignty over Lower Burma. Therefore British insisted on installing it themselves.

1872   King Mindon made other meritorious bequests to the pagoda, offering 18,000 packages of gold leaf.

1873   King Mindon erected a monastery at the eastern foot of the Pagoda Hill

1885   Board of nine trustees appointed.

1888   Earthquake brought down the vane which was repaired and re-elevated in 1889.

1898   New scheme for regulating Shwedagon Pagoda Trust is introduced and nine trustees elected by Burmese Buddhist Association of Rangoon.

1917   Resolution that footwear should be banned on pagodas, their lands and in Buddhist monasteries is passed. Although footwear prohibited by Burmese kings, after annexation of Lower Burma, the regulation was openly flouted by Europeans.

1920   Rangoon University strike students camp at foot of Pagoda Hill. Beginning of moves to oust miltary presence from the site.

1929   British troops vacate Pagoda HIll after 77 years of occupation.

1930   Western Stepway opened to Burmese public.

1930   Earthquake which brought down the Shwe Maw Daw at Bago only slightly damages the *hti*.

1931   Disastrous fire burns 21 structures and several prayer posts.

1945-46   At height of political struggle, Bogyoke Aung San uses middle terrace of Pagoda Hill as venue for many mass meetings.

1970   Earthquake of slight intensity puts shaft of *hti* out of alignment. Trustees therefore decide to make a thorough technical check of crowning structure of pagoda. The 1,362 bells suspended from the *hti* and cone were taken down and restored and their inscriptions recorded. Numerous gifts were offered at this time.

BIBLIOGRAPHY

Aung Than, U. no date (1966?) *The Golden Glory*, Shwedagon Pagoda. Directorate of Information, Rangoon.

Bhaddanta Vicittasarabhivamsa (tr. U Ko Lay and U Tin Lwin) 1992. *The Great Chronicle of Buddhas*. Yangon

Biggs, T. H. 1895. *The Shwe Dagon Pagoda*. Rangoon, Hanthawaddy Press.

Chit, Khin Myo. 1984. *A Wonderland of Burmese Legends*. Bangkok:Tamarind Press.

Courtauld, C. 1984. *In Search of Burma*. London. F. Muller Ltd.

Cowell, E.B. 1901, 1905. *The Jataka or Stories of the Buddha's Former Births*. Vol. I, IV.

Directorate of Information. n.d. *Rangoon pictorial guide*. Rangoon, Sarpay Beikaman.

Duroiselle, C. 1923-4. 'The Age of the Shwedagon Pagoda at Rangoon', pp.126-8 in *The Archaeological Survey of India Report 1923-4*.

Forchammer, E. n. d. *The Shwe Dagon*.

Fraser-Lu, S. 1994. *Burmese crafts: past and present*. Kuala Lumpur: Oxford University Press.

Furnivall, J. S. 1915. 'History of Syriam', *Journal of the Burma Research Society V*, Rangoon.

Furnivall, J. S. 1913-14. 'Notes on the History of Hanthawaddy'.*Journal of the Burma Research Society, pts.I-IV*.

Halliday, R. 1923. 'The History of [Mon] Kings', *Journal of the Burma Research Society, XIII*.

Havelock, H. 1928. *Memoirs of the Three Campaigns ... of Campbell's Army*.

Herbert, P. 1993. *The Life of the Buddha*. London: The British Library.

Htin Aung, Maung. 1959. *Folk Elements in Burmese Buddhism*. Rangoon, Dept. of Religious Affairs.

Kin Maung Nyunt. 1997. 'King Thayawaddy's Bell, "Maha Ti Sadda Ghanda" ', pp.74-77 in *Today*.

Moore, E. & Daw San San Maw 1995.'Hintha and Kinnaya, the Avian Inscpiration in Myanmar Art'. p25-31 in *Orientations. Vol. XLI no2*.

O'Connor, V.C. Scott. 1904. *The Silken East, A record of life and travel in Burma*. London: Hutchinson & Co.

Pan Hla, Nai. 1956. 'Shwe Dagon Mon Kyauksa' [the Shwe Dagon Mon Inscriptions] pp.22-4 in *Pyidaungzu Yinkyemhu vol 1*, March.

Klein, W. 1992. Insight guide, *Myanmar (Burma)*. Singapore, Hofer Press.

Pan Hla, Nai. 1985. 'Shwe Dagon hpaya Mon Kyauksa' [the Shwe Dagon Mon Inscriptions] pp.89-93 in *Ngwetayi*. May.

Pe Maung Tin. 1934. 'The Shwe Dagon Pagoda' *The Journal of the Burma Research Society, XXIV, no.1*.

Pe Maung Tin. 'New Htee for the Shwe Dagon Pagoda'. *Annual Reports on the Administration of British Burma*.

Pearn, B.R. 1939. *A History of Rangoon*. American Baptist Mission Press, Rangoon.

Shwedagon Thamaing modern chronicle of the Shwedagon.

Superintendent, Govt. Printing Office.1946. *Shwedagon, the sacred shrine*. Government Printing and Stationery, Rangoon.

Shorto, H. 1977. 'The Stupa as Buddha Icon in South East Asia', pp.75-81 in *Mahayanist Art After A.D.900*. Percival David Colloquies on Art and Archaeology in Asia no. 2 [ed. W.Watson].

Singer, N. 1993. *Burmah, a photographic Journey 1855-1925*. Stirling, Kiscadale.

Singer, N. 1995. *Old Rangoon, the city of the Shwedagon*. Stirling, Kiscadale.

Thaw Ka. 1958. 'The Early Art of Burma', pp.33-45 in *Atlantic Monthly Supplement, Perspectives of Burma*. New York.

Tun Aung Chain & Thein Hlaing. 1996. *Shwedagon*. The Universities Press. Yangon. Myanmar..

Win Pe. 1972. *Shwe Dagon*. Rangoon, Printing and Publishing Corporation.

Win Tin Win. AV Media, Yangon. *Shwedagon video*.

ACKNOWLEDGEMENTS

Much more remains to be written about the Shwedagon. It is hoped that this book will encourage both Myanmar and foreign pilgrims and visitors to seek out new corners of the pagoda.

Many people have helped me with this text, although all errors remain my own. I would like in particular to thank the following people. In Myanmar, U Nyunt Han, U Kyaw Win, Daw San San May, U Aung Myint, U Maung Maung Tin, U Win Maung (Tampawaddy), U Sein Myint, Daw Gillian Thida Moh, Miss Mandy Pearson, U Win Tin Win, and Dr Pansy Po. In London, HE U Win Aung, U Aye Ne Win, John Okell, and of course Narisa Chakrabongse and Hansjörg Mayer.

Elizabeth Moore

ADDITIONAL PHOTOGRAPHY

Lin Tin Aung and Commander Tin Aung, Elephant House: pages 102, 103 (3), 107, 108, 109, 111, 112, 113, 114, 115, 117, 121, 126, 127, 128, 130, 134, 142, 149-151, 178, 180-81

Neyla Freeman: pages 103, 127, 129, 152

Williams Hunt Collection at the School of Oriental and African Studies, University of London: page 141

India Office Collection: pages 2, 4, 6, 8, 100, 134, 135, 136, 143-48, 153-75

Office of the Pagoda Trustees: pages 182-83